AuthorHouse™ UK
1663 Liberty Drive
Bloomington, IN 47403 USA
www.authorhouse.co.uk
UK TFN: 0800 0148641 (Toll Free inside the UK)
UK Local: 02036 956322 (+44 20 3695 6322 from outside the UK)

Because of the dynamic nature of the Internet, any web addresses or links contained in this book may have changed
since publication and may no longer be valid. The views expressed in this work are solely those of the author and do
not necessarily reflect the views of the publisher, and the publisher hereby disclaims any responsibility for them.

Any people depicted in stock imagery provided by Getty Images are models,
and such images are being used for illustrative purposes only.
Certain stock imagery © Getty Images.

This book is printed on acid-free paper.

Illustrations by Connor Hattamsworth

ISBN: 978-1-6655-9072-3 (sc)
ISBN: 978-1-6655-9071-6 (e)

Library of Congress Control Number: 2021912230

Print information available on the last page.

Published by AuthorHouse 07/13/2021

authorHOUSE®

THE ORIGIN
and
FUTURE
of
MANKIND

SHAUN DOWLING

ILLUSTRATIONS BY
CONNOR HATTAMSWORTH

CONTENTS

Contents

INTRODUCTION

This book covers an amazing span of history, from the origin of the universe into far in the future. It describes how the universe was formed, how our own planet developed, when the first form of life appeared and how animal life developed over thirteen paleontological periods.

It races through the early history of mankind from hunter-gatherers to farmers, and from warlike leaders to Roman emperors, and surveys the different empires from Sumeria to the present day.

Finally, it considers what might happen in the next hundred years, and then one thousand years, then one million years, leaving the reader to consider what the future might bring.

Perhaps it all happens so quickly that you are dazzled by the speed. If so, you can always go back to the period you find most interesting and read up on all the other available sources you can find.

CHAPTER 1

THE BEGINNINGS

"Cogito ergo sum" declared the French philosopher, René Descartes, "I think therefore I am." So, if you think that you are - that you exist, and that it is not all one big dream, you have to acknowledge that you are just one part of a vast civilisation of nearly 8 billion people, living on earth, part of a solar system, one amongst trillions and trillions of stars.

So where did it all begin? What was the origin of the universe? Over the centuries there have been many theories on how the universe evolved, both secular and religious. Ancient Greek and Indian philosophers believed that the earth was the centre of the universe. As long ago as 2500 BC the Greeks thought everything in the universe was made of fundamental particles like building blocks, which later cosmologists came to view as atoms, not realising that atoms were not the smallest particle, being composed of protons, neutrons and electrons. Aristotle thought that nine concentric spheres encircled the earth, the outermost being the heavens. Later, a Greek astronomer, Claudius Ptolemy, thought that each planet moved around in small circles called epicycles, spinning round larger spheres. In the sixteenth century, Copernicus calculated that the sun was the centre of the solar system, not the earth, and all the planets orbited the sun, the earth being the third nearest, with the moon encircling the earth.

Throughout history I believe the majority of people did not bother to think about evolution at all. They followed the dictates of their religious teaching, whether from priests, shamans or theologians, and got on with their lives as best they could. Unquestionably, a religious or other spiritual belief is the simplest, most comfortable path to follow. It provides divine laws which control society. It gives meaning to life and a sense of belonging. It provides answers to the miracles of nature and consoles families for the ending of life.

It also answers the question of how life began. In the first book of Genesis, God created heaven and earth, and over six days created land, water, fruit, fishes, fowls, cattle and all the beasts of the earth. Finally, He created mankind whom He blessed on the seventh day. Hindus believe that all human and animal life were created by the deity, Brahma. Both Hindus and Buddhists believe that the creation of the universe is a continuous process, although Hindus believe that its creation is interspersed with periods of destruction - which is in line with current knowledge that the earth has gone through many critical climatic changes. According to the Koran, Moslems believe that Allah created the earth, the mountains, the heavens and the stars in six days, in accordance with Christian beliefs.

Putting the comfort of religion aside, we must now turn to the scientific theories. As recently as the 1940's, the most believable theory was that the Universe has always existed and, wherever and whenever you look, the earth, the stars, the galaxies and space are and were always the same, and will always remain the same. Thus, the universe has no beginning and no end. This is called the Steady State Theory and it is comfortable to believe in, whether true or not.

However, problems arose in the 1930's when astronomers, in particular Edwin Hubble, in measuring light from distant galaxies, found that the galaxies beyond our own, the Milky Way, were moving away from us, the farther away they are, the faster they were moving. Whilst gravity is holding individual galaxies and also our own solar system together, some form of anti-gravity is moving other galaxies farther away. This force is called 'inflation'. So, if galaxies are constantly moving away from us, we must ask ourselves, winding back in time, where did they start from in the first place. Winding time backwards to its ultimate infinite point, you get to what is called a 'singularity' when all galaxies and all matter shrink to a single point, when space and time were created and the Universe began. Cosmologists call this the Big Bang theory.

It is hard to explain how a single point at a phenomenally high temperature can expand, in a split second, as in a massive nuclear explosion, and then cool within seconds as it continues to expand. It is estimated that, from a temperature of 1,000 billion degrees Kelvin (K), the Universe, cooled to 100 billion degrees K in one hundredth of a second and then to 3 billion degrees K in 13 seconds, then to 1 billion K in 3 minutes and to 300 million K in 30 minutes. (Degrees K or Kelvin > equals degrees Celsius plus 273). It has been calculated that this occurred 13.8 billion years ago. At this point there was no matter as we understand it, only clouds of gas composed of fundamental particles of protons, neutrons and electrons. This period of inflation is estimated to have continued for 377,000 years until the gas was cool enough for atoms to form into hydrogen and helium. The decoupling of protons into atoms then caused a faint glow of radiation.

How do we know when atoms were first formed? In the 1960's astronomers were investigating microwaves beyond our galaxies when they discovered that wherever they pointed their antennae, they were picking up microwave radiation in every direction and this could be measured by a radio telescope. This is now called cosmic microwave radiation and they can measure the faint glow of radiation 377,000 years after Big Bang. Scientists are now trying to replicate this process in the CERN laboratory in Switzerland by smashing together protons and electrons in a particle accelerator.

The whole theory of the Big Bang is frankly so incredible that it is barely believable to ordinary people and raises so many questions. If there was no space or time beforehand, either nothing existed, or as some speculate, the Big Bang was one of a series of similar events when the Universe first collapsed and then started up again. But if it is proven that nothing existed or has ever existed beforehand, how could a singularity turn into an ever-expanding fireball? Perhaps the theologians were right after all. Only a divine power could have provided such a miracle - except that God did not create the world in 7 days, he created it in a split second!

If we haven't solved all the questions, we do at least know some of the answers. We do know, for example, what the universe is made of. Only a small part, 5% or so, is made of ordinary matter. Of the rest, 68% consists of dark energy and 27% of dark matter. Ordinary matter consists of atoms, gas and electrons of which ordinary stars are made, whilst only a very small amount of ordinary matter is solid matter that make up planets. There are said to be one trillion galaxies like the Milky Way in the Universe and two trillion trillion stars (that is two plus 24 noughts!) However, even that is uncertain as the number seems to increase every time an estimate is made.

In nearly every large galaxy there is a massive black hole in the centre, so dense and with such a gravitational pull that nothing dragged into it, including light, can escape. It is estimated that our own galaxy, the Milky Way, was formed about 11 billion years ago, one of 54 galaxies in the Virgo Cluster, which itself is part of the Laniakea Supercluster of galaxies, the total extending as long as 500 light years. The Milky Way itself is thought to contain over 100 solar systems like our own.

CHAPTER 2

THE SOLAR SYSTEM

Our solar system was formed around 4.6 billion years ago from the gravitational collapse and ignition of a cloud of dust and hydrogen, and could also have developed from the debris of older stars. Our sun is 100 times the diameter of the earth, burning at about 15 billion degrees K at the centre and 6000 billion degrees K on the surface. Every second it gives off 400 billion billion watts of energy. However, like all stars, our sun will eventually run out of fuel. In about 5 billion years it will explode in a flash, turn into a red giant and cool into a cinder. That would be one obvious end to mankind which we discuss in later chapters.

So long as our sun does exist, it will continue to run with eight different planets circling round in an elliptical orbit, together with their own moons, and also a mass of asteroids, rocks and ice. Our own planet earth orbits the sun in 365½ days, whilst Saturn, with its 62 moons, takes nearly 30 years to orbit the sun. Neptune, the farthest away, is 2.8 billion miles from the sun.

Our own planet earth is the densest of the planets. It did not evolve from dust and gas in a gravitational collapse like stars, but grew from small beginnings, bombarded by rocks, ice-comets and asteroids, spinning round and growing larger in stages, pulled together by gravity. It finally evolved around 4.5 billion years ago, cooling down to form a thin crust with a mantel below, still continuously bombarded with asteroids and rocks up to 3.8 billion years ago in what is known as the Late Heavy Bombardment. Our moon was formed shortly afterwards, possibly from an asteroid clash with earth.

The inner core of earth is solid but it is surrounded by an outer core of intensely hot magma. Around 3.5 billion years ago the crust split up into continental plates, largely covered with water which are now our oceans. There are various theories about where the water came from, but the majority view is that it came from ice-comets. These continental plates slide around slowly on the upper mantel, sometimes crashing into another plate, subverting their edges, causing earthquakes, volcanoes and hydrothermal vents with magma flowing to the surface.

The surface of the earth is protected by an outer atmosphere which shields us from the sun's radiation. The first atmosphere, mainly hydrogen and helium, was blown away by a solar wind and replaced by a more stable atmosphere consisting of water vapour, carbon dioxide, nitrogen, methane and other gasses, but with little or no oxygen. It wasn't until later photosynthesis that vegetation, capturing photons beamed from the sun, absorbed carbon dioxide and gave off oxygen which is essential for life.

We probably do not realise that tectonic plates continue sliding around right up to the present day. About 300 million years ago there was one large plate called Pangea, stretching from the north to the south pole, but by 175 million years ago, it had split into the Laurentia plate in the north and the Gondwana plate in the south, with a vast Panthalassic Ocean on one side and the Tethys Ocean on the other *(see figure 1).* Bit by bit it broke off into what is now North America, South America and Europe, creating the Atlantic Ocean. This continuous motion, particularly on the plate boundaries, caused massive upheavals with mountain ranges thrown up and deep rifts occurring. A good example is the East African Rift which stretches from Ethiopia to Mozambique, creating the Gulf and the Red Sea and changing the climate from afforestation to desert, which, as we shall see later, led to the development of biped hominins. The volcanic activity at the tectonic plate boundaries along the Rift also created fertile agricultural land on which early man thrived.

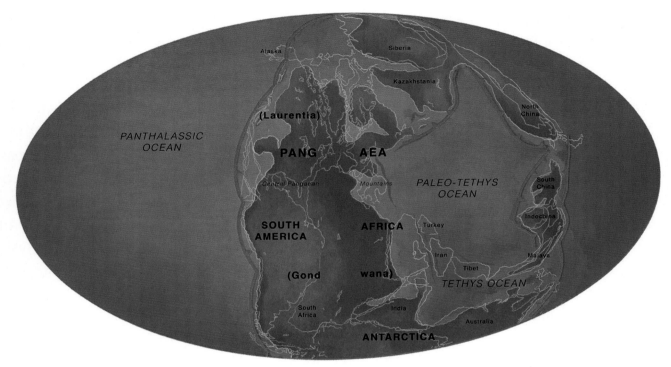

Figure 1: Pangea

From the north pole to the south, climate conditions alternated from hot and humid to freezing cold, with vast glaciers creeping over the land mass, raising and lowering sea levels. From 4 billion years ago, the sea level has been as much as 300 metres higher, severely reducing the total land area and changing continental boundaries. When the sea level was 100 metres lower, early man could reach neighbouring lands and islands on foot.

Looking at rock formation, there is little left of the earth's crust 4 million years ago that we can still see, as so much of the land was subverted under the mantle and covered with magma extrusions. The hardest rock we can see today is volcanic or igneous rock like granite, derived from solidified magma and then exposed as mountain ranges are eroded away over time. Sandstone, compressed from other materials, is much easier to work. The most interesting sedimentary rock is called biological rock, formed from the sedimentation and compression of fossils and sea shells, from which we can examine the earliest forms of life.

Diverging for a minute from planet earth to our fellow planet Mars, which is only half our size and emerged at the same time as earth, its rocky terrain is fairly similar to ours although its volcanic mountains are twice as high as Everest and its canyons are four times as deep. At one time it was thought that water poured over water courses there in the past and their present clouds may be formed from icy particles. Unfortunately, its magnetic field was very weak, the atmosphere got swept away, the planet froze and the water dried out. It is quite possible that there was early life, similar to ours, and various probes are currently being sent there to find out, and, if possible, bring rock samples back for analysis. On earth, some of the oldest evidence shows that colonies of microbes grew layer upon layer in shallow water and there is no reason why, before the atmosphere was swept away, microbes could not have survived on Mars.

At the moment, we are only looking at one planet. If there are two trillion trillion stars in the Universe and many of them, like the sun, will also have planets, then the chance of life on one of them must be highly likely. The only problem is they are all so far away, that, even with the development of space travel and assuming that "unidentified flying objects" do not exist, we humans may never be able to reach them.

We have also just heard that phosphine gas has been found round the planet Venus and that microbial life might be up there in the clouds. Whether likely or not, it is not really relevant as the temperature on Venus is around 465°C, so no animal or human life could survive there.

CHAPTER 3

LIFE ON EARTH

Turning back to earth, we need to see how life developed after the Late Heavy Bombardment. The best way to do this is to follow a series of paleontological periods, starting with the Precambrian period from four billion to 541 million years ago (or to abbreviate, mya). This timescale allows geologists to construct an accurate internationally recognised chronology of evolution, allowing them to check the dates of ancient fossils, using radiometric dating.

A list of the periods

The following is a list of paleontological periods and the range of ages in millions of years ago (mya) :

- o   Precambrian   4,600 – 541 mya

- o   Cambrian   541 – 485.4 mya

- o   Ordovician   485.4 – 443.8 mya – ending with the first major extinction

- Silurian   443.8 – 419.2 mya

- Devonian   419.2 – 358.9 mya – ending with the second major extinction

- Carboniferous   358.9 – 298.9 mya

- Permian   298.9 – 251.902 mya – ending with the third major extinction

- Triassic   251.9 – 201.3 mya – ending with the fourth major extinction

- Jurassic   201.3 – 145 mya

- Cretaceous   145 – 66 mya – ending with the fifth major extinction

- Paleogene   66 – 23.03 mya

- Neogene   23.03 – 2.58 mya

- Quaternary   2.58 mya to the present day

Precambrian Period 4,000 – 541 mya

As we saw earlier, the first atmosphere of nitrogen, methane and carbon dioxide, plus high temperatures, was not conducive to life, although the temperature cooled after 2.500 mya. The earliest fossils may have been laid down as far back as 4 billion mya and there is evidence that early forms of bacteria existed 3.5 mya. Stromatolites could then be found spreading over volcanic rock surfaces, as oxygen levels started to rise. Stromatolites are classed as colonies of cyanobacteria, or single cell prokaryotes. Fossils have been found on sedimentary rocks containing sheets of stromatolite microbes, layered one on top of another, surviving and growing by photosynthesis. They are an important first step as prokaryotes lead on to the most important development of all time, the birth of eukaryotes - although some scientists believe that both prokaryotes and eukaryotes emerged side by side.

Prokaryotes have their own DNA and protein, but do not have a nucleus or mitochondria, which produce energy. Hence, they have to use photosynthesis for energy. Eukaryotes are the most important cells for the development of life. They make up plants and all species of animals, including ourselves. Our own bodies contain at least one trillion eukaryotic cells (*figure 2*). Each has a permeable membrane containing cytoplasm, a nucleus, tiny organs (or organelles) and mitochondria. Inside the nucleus there are thousands of chromosomes (*figure 3*), made up of DNA molecules, each arranged in a double helix like a long-twisted ladder. Our DNA can now be read, it can tell us about our history and can be used for medical diagnosis. The mitochondria are all-important for respiration and the production of energy, without which no animal would survive. The first eukaryote cells were known to exist 1.7 billion years ago although some scientists say it might be much earlier. The first eukaryotic multicellular plant was green algae, found about one billion years ago, followed by seaweed about 800 mya.

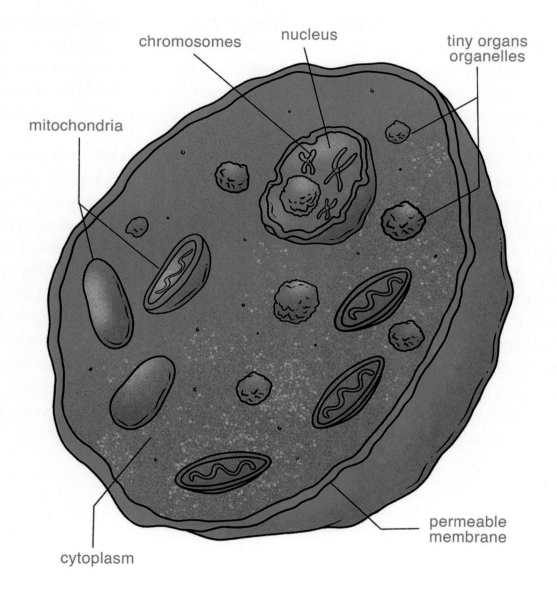

mitochondria

chromosomes

nucleus

tiny organs
organelles

cytoplasm

permeable
membrane

Figure 2: Eukaryotic Cell

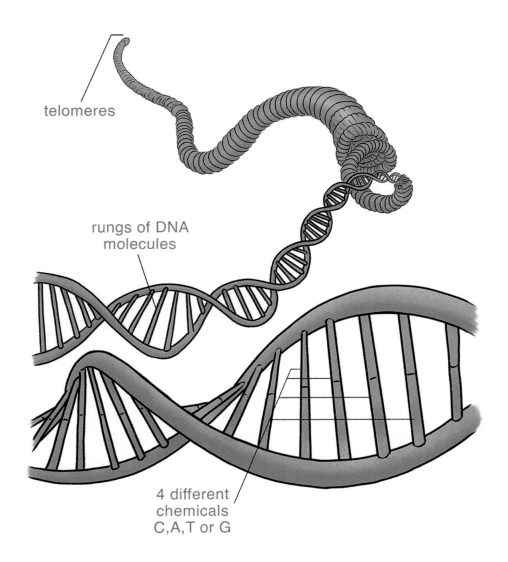

telomeres

rungs of DNA molecules

4 different chemicals C,A,T or G

Figure 3: Chromosomes

Evolution speeded up at the end of the Precambrian period. Multicellular eukaryotes, the Dickinsonia species, found in fossils dated from 571 mya, were oval, symmetric and segmented, ranging from a few millimetres to over a metre long. There were also Haootia, fibrous muscular invertebrates that arrived 560 mya (*figure 4*). These were followed by chordates from 540 mya (*figure 5*) which were marine filter feeders with fish shapes, each having a mouth but no jaws, a notochord (a stiff rod of cartilage), a nerve cord (that later became a spinal cord) and a tail fin. By 520 mya they were followed by tiny Trilobites, arthropods with a segmented body encased in a calcite shell, with a head, eyes, legs, gills and spines, feeding on organic matter on the sea floor.

Cambrian Period 541 – 485 mya

In the Cambrian period, 85 per cent of the globe was oceanic, sea levels were high and a lot of the land was flooded. Temperature levels averaged over 50°C and carbon dioxide levels were high too, over ten times as high as today. But the period did see an acceleration of vertebrate and invertebrate development, sometimes called the Cambrian explosion.

Following the trilobites, other species came along including shelly molluscs, sea anemones, corals, jelly fish and plankton by 500 mya. There were tiny *Marella* less than an inch long, with well-developed crab like claws and twenty thin feathered legs, whilst the *Anomalocaris* (*figure 6*) grew to one metre long with protruding eyes and long claws, like a shrimp, which fed on smaller shell fish. One bizarre shaped fish which arrived at about the same time was an *Opabinia*, two or three inches long, with fifteen segments, five eyes and a protruding hollow proboscis. The first vertebrates appeared this time like fish with a spinal cord, mouth, eyes, a brain and sensory organs, but still no jaws. However, in 500 mya oxygen levels fell and hydrogen sulphide increased, causing the extinction of all the vertebrates, apart from lampreys, which can still be found in rivers and seas.

Figure 4: Haootia

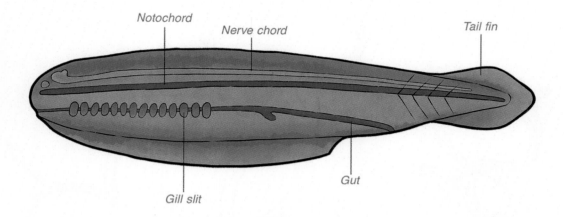

Notochord   Nerve chord   Tail fin

Gill slit   Gut

Figure 5: Chordate

Figure 6: Anomalocaris

Ordovician Period 485 – 444 mya

The southern tectonic plates, or continents, merged into Gondwana and moved slowly south. Sea levels started high but fell back during the period. An enormous number of meteorites continued to bombard the earth. The temperature was warm at the onset but by the end of the period it was the coldest for 600 million years. Spiny trilobites like *Selenopeltis* (*figure* 7) managed to flourish, whilst invertebrate molluscs and arthropods dominated the oceans and various fungi developed on land. The first jawed fish appeared. But another mass extinction, the second largest, wiped out most of the trilobite and conodont species.

Silurian Period 444 – 419 mya

The climate was warm but variable with intermittent ice ages. Some of the land consisted of island chains (*figure* 8) covered with fresh water plants. Fish now developed jaws, enabling them to eat both smaller animals whilst some invertebrates like *Pseudocrinites* (*figure* 9) anchored themselves to the sea floor, picking up food as the water swelled past.

Devonian Period 419 – 339 mya

This period saw considerable movement of tectonic plates, with changing boundaries, surrounded by vast oceans. Sea levels were high and much land lay under shallow seas. The climate was warm and dry with little glaciation at the poles. Carbon dioxide levels continued to fall.

Figure 7: Senenopeltis

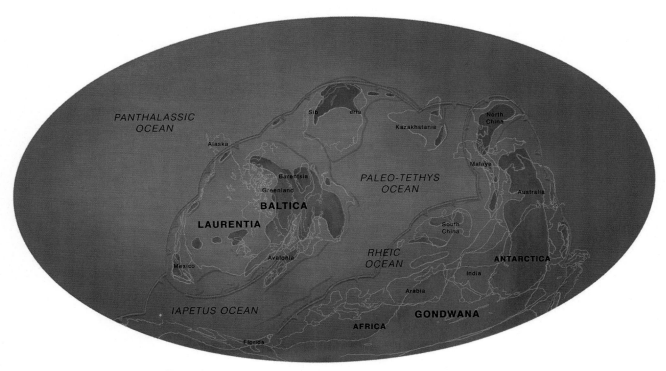

Figure 8: Island Chains

Figure 9: Pseudocrinites

All kinds of plants, algae, moss, ferns, seed plants, horse tails and early tree types spread over the land, developing roots, leaves and lateral branches, which led eventually to forests. One column-like fungus rose as high as twenty feet, towering over the vegetation below. Many varieties of fish appeared, like the *Rolfosteus* (**figure 10**), with more varied shapes than fish today as nature appeared to be experimenting with the most effective marine animals.

The most evolutionary development in the late Devonian period was the beginning of early tetrapods (four-legged vertebrates) as fish with gills used their fins to slither along muddy river banks and crawl onto land for short periods of time. Fossils reveal that these leg-like fins had five digits at the end, which were to become fingers or toes. However, most of this species was wiped out in several mass extinctions around 372 mya.

Carboniferous Period 359 – 299 mya

The Carboniferous (carbon-bearing) period was so named as swamps laid down huge coal deposits. At this time the two continents, Euro America and Gondwana, started to merge into one supercontinent, Pangea. The warmer climate in central regions with rising sea levels led to flooding of coastal swamps, although glaciers developed at the poles. On land, rising oxygen levels and falling carbon dioxide spurred growth of vegetation and animals alike. Greater forestation with an abundance of tall trees, provided cover for early reptiles. On land, small invertebrates like millipedes with segmented bodies, burrowed under the vegetation. At sea, sharks proliferated in an unusual variety of shapes.

The first tetrapods were amphibian but developed into reptiles with proper legs, laying their eggs on the ground, gradually becoming more like baby crocodiles. One of the biggest, the *Ophiacodon* (**figure 11**) was up to ten feet long, had a large scaly body and sharp teeth, lived on river banks and ate only fish. At the end of the period there was another extinction when the climate became cold and arid. Some glaciation occurred and tropical rainforests actually collapsed.

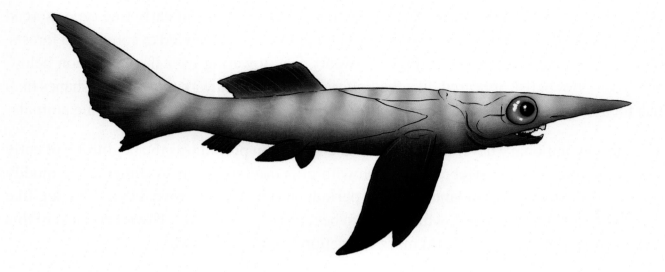

Figure 10: Rolfosteus

Figure 11: Ophiacodon

Permian Period 299 – 252 mya

The land mass was dominated by the supercontinent Pangea. Starting with an ice age, the land warmed up, drying out the swamps, and conifer trees first appeared. Insects flourished, mostly like cockroaches, but some like dragonflies took to the skies. On land, mammal like reptiles with thick skins, fierce-looking jaws, serrated teeth and sturdy legs underneath their bodies (not splayed out) dominated the animal kingdom. One common animal, the *Dimetrodon* (*figure 12*), a synapsid, had a tall, scaly sail back, with strong legs, well developed jaws and eighty pointed teeth.

At the end of the period the first lizard-like reptile, an archosauriform, appeared, the forerunner of dinosaurs. However, this was not to last as the biggest ever extinction occurred at the end of the Permian period and the beginning of the Triassic period, when it is said that 95 per cent of marine animals and 70 per cent of land animals, even insects, were wiped out. The evidence seems to be that the mass extrusion of magma onto the land, together with high volcanic activity, raised levels of carbon dioxide and the oceans vented sulphur dioxide, although palaeontologists still dispute the causes.

Triassic Period 252 – 201 mya

The first 20 to 30 million years of the Triassic period was spent recovering from the Permian-Triassic extinction. The climate was hot and dry, with no glaciation, although the polar regions were moist, which was good for ferns, seed plants and small tufted trees. The lakes and rivers were populated by lungfish and other amphibians.

On land the main vertebrates were archosaurs, warm blooded mammal-like reptiles with a sprawling gait (as they had sideways facing hip sockets) and therapsids, more powerful mammals with an upright stance, vertically positioned legs, large heads and powerful jaws. Of the three main groups of archosaurs, birds, crocodilians and dinosaurs, only birds and crocodiles remain today.

Figure 12: Dimetrodon

Dinosaurs were not so big in the Triassic period although one predator, the *Postosuchus* (**figure 13**) grew up to fifteen feet long, with a barrel shaped body, powerful jaws and a tail to balance. One Pterosaur (**figure 14**), a flying reptile, the *Eudimorphodon*, was as big as an eagle, with elongated fingers supporting the front wing membrane and with small reptile type teeth for eating prey, probably better at gliding than flying. Another extinction occurred at the end of the period, although not as bad as the first.

Figure 13: Postosuchus

Figure 14: Eudimorphodon

Jurassic Period 201 – 145 mya

As the Pangea supercontinent rifted apart, splitting into Laurentia in the North and Gondwana in the south, there were two more extinctions in the period, one early Jurassic and one at the end. The climate was hotter and more humid, encouraging forests and speeding up the evolution of animals. Dinosaurs, both herbivore and carnivore, dominated the land getting bigger and heavier, and the oceans were inhabited by ichthyosaurs. Pterosaurs became the dominant flying vertebrates one of which, the *Pterodactylus (figure 15)* is probably the best known, whilst the *Archaeopterix (figure 16)* with long wings and tail feathers is regarded as the first modern bird.

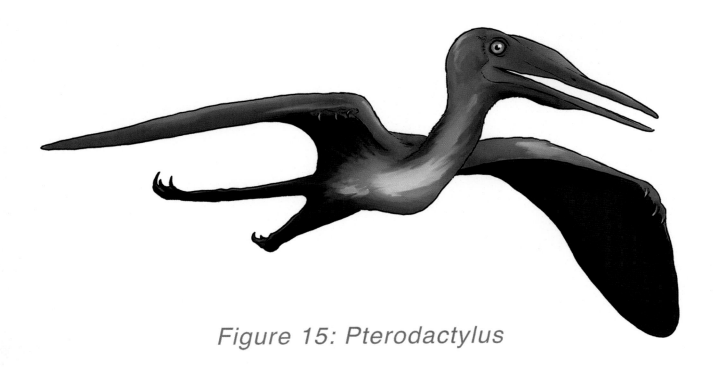

Figure 15: Pterodactylus

Figure 16: Archaeopteryx

Amongst the many dinosaurs, the *Brachiosaurus* **(figure 17),** with long legs and a long neck, weighed up to fifty tons and stretched eighty feet, head to tail, tall enough to eat the treetops. The *Diplodocus* was also nearly eighty feet long, but with a long neck and very long tail it weighed only sixteen tons. One of the dinosaurs, the *Kentrosaurus* **(figure 18),** which had two rows of plates and spikes along its back, is classed as a stegosaurus (plated lizard) and may have lived in herds.

The largest fish, a *Leedsichthys*, was up to fifty-five feet long. It was a filter feeder with thousands of teeth, but not a predator. The smaller *Stenopterygius* was only ten feet long, but it could swim at up to sixty miles per hour!

Cretaceous Period 145 – 66 mya

This period was named after the deposit of more chalk than in any other period. Ocean sea levels were at their highest, creating numerous shallow inland seas. Whilst the Gondwana continent remained intact, what are now South America, Australia and the Antarctic drifted away from Africa. The climate started off cold, with some glaciation, but warmed up as the period went on, although the temperature oscillated every few million years. In some places the outpouring of magma raised carbon dioxide levels.

On land, flowers appeared pollinated by the first bees. At sea, rays and sharks of various sizes proliferated. And closer to land, there were masses of clams, scallops and shellfish. Later in the period a giant marine predator, the *Mosasaurus* **(figure 19)** arrived, nearly fifty feet long, slim, with wide flippers and enormous jaws to rival the sharks.

There were lots of small birds, more like today, but one giant pterosaur, an *Ornithocheirus*, had a wingspan of sixteen feet, whilst later in the period an even bigger bird, a *Quetzalcoatlus* **(figure 20)** arrived with a wingspan of thirty-nine feet. It was a fierce predator with strong pointed jaws, a long neck and an unusually long body.

Figure 17: Brachiosaurus

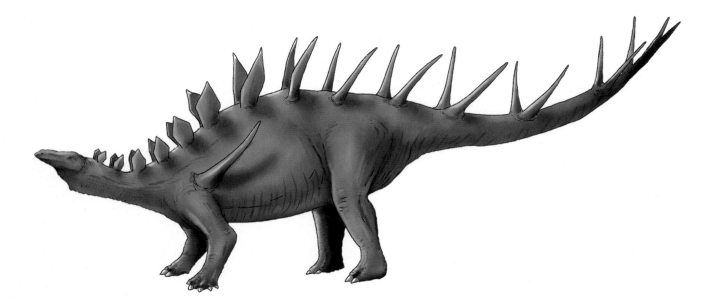

Figure 18: Kentrosaurus

Figure 19: Mosasaurus

Figure 20: Quetzalcoatlus

Pride of place were the dinosaurs, both large and small. One large heavyweight with a scaly back and lethal shoulder spikes was the *Edmontonia (figure 21)*. The *Spinosaurus (figure 22),* nearly fifty feet long with a scaly humped back, hunted not only on land but also in the water. The most famous dinosaur was, of course, *Tyrannosaurus Rex*. Not the biggest, only forty feet long, it was fast moving with two long legs and a tail balancing its body *(figure 23)*. It was allegedly the fiercest predator with a big brain, a large jaw, a strong bite and fifty-eight teeth, swallowing its victims, bones and all. Another well-known dinosaur, only twenty-three feet long, a *Triceratops*, walked on four legs. Despite having a six-foot long head, a huge jaw and two massive horns, it was just a harmless herbivore.

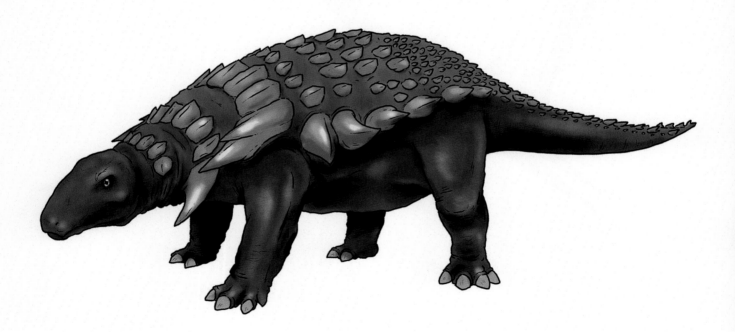

Figure 21: Edmontonia

Figure 22: Spinosaurus

Figure 23: Tryannosaurus Rex

However, the age of the dinosaur was not to last. In 66 mya the earth was struck by a number of asteroids, the largest hitting the Yucatán peninsula in Mexico, penetrating the crust and creating a crater over six miles wide. The explosion was equal to over a hundred times the power of an atom bomb, incinerating forests in its path. It clouded the skies with vaporised rock, ash and gasses. This is said to have lasted for two years, and all plants dependent on photosynthesis died off. Some scientists think that outpouring of magma from heightened volcanic action choked the air with carbon dioxide, which would have had a similar effect as the asteroids.

Whatever happened, the herbivores died off first, and then the carnivores. Marine animals survived the best and many crocodilians survived as well. Some bird species survived. But in total, three quarters of all plants and animals were wiped out.

Paleogene Period 66 – 23 mya

During this period the continents continued to separate and new mountain ranges appeared. Temperatures oscillated from hot, dry and humid to cold and dry, particularly towards the end of the period. Vast deciduous forests spread over the land and new grasses evolved which helped all grazing animals.

After the dominance, and then the extinction of the dinosaurs, you can find the earliest ancestors of whales, elephants and hoofed mammals. Birds proliferated, both flying and flightless, like the six-foot *Gastornis* (*figure 24*). The first primates appeared with large brains, proper vision and dexterous hands. One sub order, the simians, a monkey and ape group, appeared around 40 mya. Around 25 mya the simians split into two groups, Old World monkeys (baboons, gibbons and macaques) and apes (orangutans, gorillas and chimpanzees). This last group, is the most important, as we shall see below, when hominins and chimpanzees developed side by side.

Neogene Period 23 – 2 mya

The tectonic plates had just about finished sliding about but subversions still threw up new mountain ranges. Temperatures dropped, as did sea levels, and poles iced over. Lower sea levels allowed two land bridges to appear, one from Africa to Asia, and the other from Asia to North America. Grassland replaced many forests on which herds of bison and horses grazed together as did other ungulates like cattle, sheep, tapirs and rhinoceroses.

At sea, new whale and shark species developed. The largest predatory shark, the *Carcharocles*, nearly sixty feet long, weighing fifty tons, sporting big jaws, large teeth and a strong bite, terrorised the seas (*figure 25*).

The giant rhinoceros was the tallest land animal, whilst the largest bird, the *Argentavis* (*figure 26*) had an eight-metre wingspan.

Figure 24: Gastornis

Figure 25: Carcarocles

Figure 26: Argentavis

CHAPTER 4

HUMAN EVOLUTION

The big event in the Neogene Period was the arrival of the hominin species, which split off from gorillas in 6 mya, and then in 4 mya divided into two species, chimpanzees (including bonobos) and australopithecines, as we can see from the diagram below:-

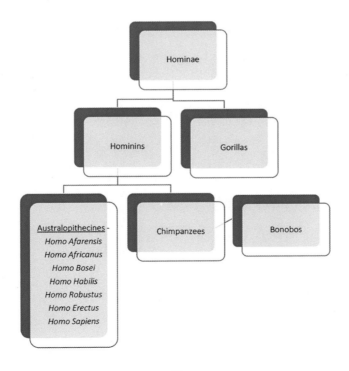

There were a number of different australopithecines over the last 4.4 million years, walking on two legs, of varying height and with a brain size between 300 and 1400 cubic centimetres. Some are thought to be the ancestors of *homo sapiens* who moved out from Africa as far as Indonesia and China. The table below shows the evolutionary development of the australopithecines from the first two main species, *homo anamensis* and *homo afarensis*, who lived alongside each other for a brief period. But there are still doubts about the first, *homo ramidus*, who some palaeontologists believe was closer to a chimpanzee and lived partly in the trees.

Date Mya	Species of *homo*	Height	Brain size in cu^3
4.4	*ramidus*	3'10"	300-350
4.2-3.8	*anamensis*	DK	370
3.9-2.9	*afarensis*	4'11"	446
	* *afarensis* 'Lucy' (female)		similar
3.7-2.0	*africanus*	4'7"	420-510
	* *africanus* 'Little Foot'		
3.5-3.3	*deyiremeda*	DK	DK
3.3-1.6	*habilis*	4'10"	500-900

2.6-2.5	*garhi*	4'7"	450
2.3-1.5	*sediba*	4'11"	420-440
2.3-1.0	*boisei*	5'1"	450-550
2.1-0.6	*robustus*	4'4"	476
1.7-1.4	*erectus*	5'3" – 6'	700-1300
700,000-200,000	*heidelbergensis*	up to 6'	1100-1400
700,000-50,000	*floresiensis*	3'7"	380
500,000 to present	*sapiens*	5' to 6'	up to 2000

(DK =
Don't Know)

(* = see below)

You can see, in very general terms, that the *australopithecus* species is generally getting taller with a bigger brain size as time goes on. *Anamensis* had a brain size similar to a bonobo, so we can see that the two cousins shown in the evolutionary tree above, the australopithecines and the chimpanzees, were not all that far apart. The smallest of the species, the *floresiensis*, with a similar brain size came along as recently as 700,000 years ago and lived until 50,000 years ago or, as some believe, much more recently, on the island of Flores in Indonesia. Sophisticated tools have been found alongside their bones which shows that brain size is not the only indicator of ability. *Floresiensis* has since been nicknamed 'The Hobbit' after the book by J. R. R. Tolkien!

The two best known preserved skeletons are of 'Lucy', a female *afarensis*, which can be seen in the Museum of Ethiopia in Addis Ababa, and *africanus* 'Little Foot', found in the Sterkfontein caves near Johannesburg and can be seen there in a museum called The Cradle of Humanities.

Meanwhile, the gorilla family carried on as a distinct species, with much bigger bodies than today, like the *Gigantopithecus (figure 27)*. One smaller ape, the *Dryopithecus (figure 28)*, was only the size of a monkey, which could walk on four legs, but mainly lived in the trees.

Quaternary Period 2.6 mya to now

We are almost home. Whilst there was periodic glaciation in the Quaternary Period, there were interglacial periods, the most recent from 12,000 years ago up to today. This affected all animal and plant life. Some animals developed thicker coats. Large animals abounded, including a giant sloth, the *Megatherium*, twenty feet long, a *woolly mammoth (figure 29)*, that stood sixteen feet tall, weighing eight tons, and a deer, the *Megalosaurus* with ten-foot antlers *(figure 30)*.

One interesting weather event occurred 75,000 years ago when there was a super-volcanic eruption at Lake Toba in Indonesia. This sent a blanket of volcanic ash over land and sea, from India to South China. This was the last of four major volcanic eruptions and may have lowered the temperature for up to a thousand years and caused a decline in the population. This is a reminder of the risks to civilisation which we cover in later chapters.

Figure 27: Gigantopithecus

Figure 28: Dryopithecus

Figure 29: Woolly Mammoth

Figure 30: Megalocerus

Amongst the hominins, there are running disputes about which *australopithecus* was really our ancestor. It is generally thought that *africanus* was the ancestor of *habilis* and that *habilis* was the ancestor of *erectus*. It was then *erectus* who led on to *homo heidelbergensis*, the Neanderthals, the Denisovans and ourselves. *Erectus (figure 31)* was certainly tall, with a human gait, a flat face, prominent nose and a brain size of 700 – 1200 cu3, compared to *sapiens* with a brain size of up to 2000 cu3. *Erectus* used tools, made fire, and is thought to have cooked and possibly used some form of communication. Some *erectus* footprints indicate that they lived in a social community and did not necessarily live in a cave. They are also known to have been able to build a shelter with a roof.

Homo heidelbergensis, the Denisovans and the Neanderthals

As we get closer to *sapiens*, what do we know about *homo heidelbergensis (figure 32),* the Denisovans and the Neanderthals? *Heidelbergensis* males were as tall as we are, with a brain size up to 1400 cu3. They lived mainly in Ethiopia, Namibia and Southern Africa and are said to be able to use spears. Studies have shown that they were also expert in shaping cutting tools. They were taller than the Denisovans and the Neanderthals and are thought to be our nearest ancestors. They had some auditory sensitivity and therefore may have been capable of some speech, if only to give warnings and communicate wishes or instructions.

The Denisovans ranged over Asia, and skeletons have been found in Russia and China. The earliest Denisovans are known to have lived from 1.3 mya and may have lived as recently as 14,500 years ago in New Guinea. It is thought they split off from the Neanderthals about 600,000 years ago. A group of five skeletons were found in a Denisovan cave in Russia together with many different stone and bone tools, as well as ornaments. It is known that they interbred with *sapiens* as Papuans have 6 per cent of their DNA and Australian aboriginals have three to five per cent. They are also known to have interbred with the Neanderthals. However, little is known of Denisovans' anatomy as so few skeletal remains have been found.

Figure 31: Homo Erectus

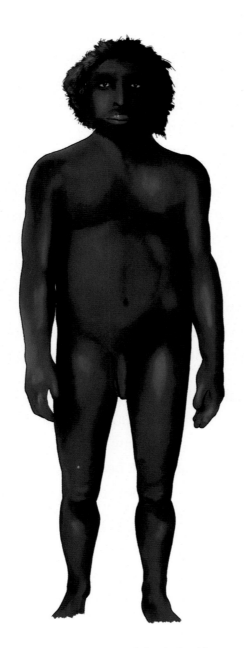

Figure 32: Homo Heidelbergensis

We know a lot more about the Neanderthals *(figure 33)* but their origins are uncertain, as is their relationship with the Denisovans. The oldest skeleton we have found only goes back to 430,000 years ago. They were more robust, squatter and had shorter legs and arms than the Heidelbergensis. The males were about five-foot-five, and the females stood around five feet tall. Their brain size is estimated at 1500 cu3. They lived in social groups of ten to thirty but most of them died before they were 40, many from injuries in hunting.

The Neanderthals were more capable than originally believed, using tools, cooking, storing food, sewing, weaving, making ornaments, using medicinal plants, treating injuries using splints and re-setting bones. They spoke, but probably could not use all of the sounds we use today. They painted, used ochre on their bodies, and buried their dead, whether or not accompanied by some form of ritual worship. They hunted big game, mainly hoofed animals, and ate meat, fish, plants and mushrooms. They were even able to fish on reed boats. They are known to have made flutes from hollow bones, so they could have played some music. So, given all their talents, history has not treated them very kindly.

There was only a small population of Neanderthals, mostly spread round the Mediterranean. However, they died out as recently as 28,000 years ago in Gibraltar, after giving *sapiens* 2-4 per cent of their DNA from interbreeding. Many ask why they died out, as they seem to have been very capable. There may have been several reasons - too small a population, inbreeding, low fertility levels, icy weather, disease, shortage of food, or conflict with *sapiens*. I doubt if we will ever know.

Figure 33: Neanderthal

Homo sapiens

Finally, we come to *homo sapiens*, who may have arrived as early as 500,000 years ago, but we only have fossils from 300,000 years ago. We know that those who were anatomically similar to ourselves only go back to 200,000 years ago. In terms of *sapiens'* modern behaviour, it is thought that this only goes back 50,000 years - that is to say, before the Neanderthals and Denisovans died out.

Behaviourally, modern *sapiens* was capable of speech, making tools and using both rafts and boats. We could cook and preserve food, domesticate sheep, goats, pigs and keep dogs for both herding and protection. We could build shelters and sew hides and skins for warmth, as the peak of the last ice age occurred 20,000 years ago and the planet did not warm up until about 15,000 BC. Paintings in the caves of Lascaux in France and others in Columbia both date back to 20,000 BC, whilst pottery that dates back to 16,000 BC was found in Xianrendong in China.

Homo sapiens migrated out of Africa around 70,000 years ago, firstly to the Middle East, and then to Asia, then to Europe, then to Australia and finally to America across the Bering Strait, about 40,000 years ago.

Hunter-Gatherers

Hunter-gatherers have been around at least since *homo erectus* and evolved over time, according to species, location, climate and temperature. Mostly they were nomadic, or semi-nomadic. Men did most of the hunting, also scavenging dead animals, while women gathered firewood, plants, eggs, fruit and small animals. As for their lifestyle, their main aim would have been to provide shelter, warmth and food, and to breed and nurture their children.

According to studies of recent hunter-gatherers, including Australian aborigines, pygmies from the Congo, tribes in New Guinea and Papua, bushmen in the Kalahari Desert and Indians in North America, hunters did not go out every day and it is thought they only hunted three times a week.

A recent study of the Ju/'hoansi tribesmen in South Africa showed they only worked fifteen hours a week and shared their provisions equally. The women would spend between two and five hours a day working, but would still have sufficient time for rearing children and cooking. Both sexes would help each other, building shelters, shaping tools, making nets and baskets, building rafts and canoes for fishing, and dealing with injuries. Socialising, singing, dancing and telling stories would occupy many evenings and nights.

Many tribes would observe rituals, burying the dead, and may have worshipped their ancestors. As the population increased, small groups of families merged into bands and tribes, which were less egalitarian, often under the control of a headman or tribal chief. If there was competition for scarce resources, this could sometimes lead to armed conflict between tribes.

The Neolithic Revolution

From 15,000 BC the ice-age ended and as the climate warmed up, it became drier. By 12,000 BC the Neolithic agricultural revolution began. Forests receded and wild grasses spread. No-one is quite certain when cereals became widespread but it started by collecting grass seeds and scattering them on the soil. Hunter-gatherers had been collecting grass seeds for thousands of years but there was no evidence until 17,000 BC that they were being ground up for eating. We do know that barley was cultivated from at least 9000 BC. The first plants for human use were wild wheat, rye, barley, flaxseeds, chickpeas, lentils, millet and maize, all of which could be sifted, ground for use or stored for winter and lean times. This led to a diet higher in carbohydrates, with less protein and fibre. As a result, the average height of male adults shrank from five foot ten to five foot six. With weaker bodies, the Neolithic families would have been more prone to diseases like flu, measles and small pox.

The most important group to emerge around 12,000 BC were the Natufians who lasted until 500 BC. They were the bridge between the hunter-gatherers and the agrarians as they continued hunting but also created settlements of over a hundred people. The remains of dwellings and decorated bodies have recently been excavated. The first and best-known settlement was a village named Jericho in Jordan. This was followed by more villages south of the Dead Sea and up the River Jordan towards what is now Syria.

Early Natufians lived in mudbrick dwellings with brushwood roofs. Later, they built dry stone walls sunk below ground level, as wide as six metres round, with a central fireplace. Very smoky! They also built defences round their settlements. They made sickles for cutting cereals, harpoons and fish hooks. They were able to make a form of pita bread and could brew beer. The Natufians buried their dead with ornaments and grave goods, and worshipped their ancestors. It is thought they held animist beliefs - that is to say, animals, plants and objects had a spiritual or supernatural essence.

Animals were plentiful up to 10,700 BC, but the climate then cooled in what is called the Younger Dryas event, lasting a thousand years, and many animals became extinct.

From 8500 BC onwards, farming became widespread in Syria, Mesopotamia and Turkey, as Natufians slashed and burnt vegetation to provide fertile land. Similar agricultural revolutions took place along the Yangtze river in China, producing rice, and also along the Indus Valley. But the changes were very gradual, dependent on location, climate and local tradition. Not all hunter gatherers became agrarians. For example, hunter-gathering continued in Central Africa right up to 5000 BC.

Lifestyle would also change only very slowly, but in due course stone buildings, thatched roofs and long houses came along, providing better protection. Cooking methods, tool-making and better pottery evolved and a wider variety of plants and fruits became available. From 7000 BC onwards, villages became larger, and then developed into towns. The first recorded town was Çatalhöyük in Cappadocia in Turkey, followed by Eridu, Ur and Uruk in Mesopotamia.

Whilst trading, or local exchange, is known to have gone on for at least 100,000 years, the advent of metals in 4000 BC at the beginning of the Bronze Age would have boosted trade, particularly around the Mediterranean, where the Phoenicians were active. The first long-distance trading recorded in the third millennium BC was from Sumer to the Harappan civilisation in the Indus Valley. This would have included not only ornaments, jewellery and foodstuffs, but metals like bronze, first smelted from copper and tin around 3500 BC.

We have now reached a point in the evolution of mankind during which hundreds of developments have occurred in different countries from 5500 BC to the present day. However, it would be quite impossible in one book to cover all these developments in each country. So, in the next chapter, I have chosen to summarise the achievements of the principal civilisations which followed, one by one, from the Sumerian Empire in 5500 BC right up to the end of the British Empire in the twentieth century.

CHAPTER 5

THE PRINCIPAL CIVILISATIONS FROM 5500 BC

Sumer

Sumer was centred in Mesopotamia, located between two rivers, Tigris and Euphrates, where the soil was extremely fertile. Where the Suma people came from is still disputed, whether from eastern Turkey, North Africa or other parts of the Levant. Settled between 5500 BC and 4000 BC, Sumer was divided into city states with walled defences. The Sumerians drained the swamps, and built dykes, canals and reservoirs. The biggest city was Uruk with a population thought to be over 50,000. Their society was male dominated and split into two groups - freemen and slaves. They believed in several gods, in human form, and their king priests offered libations to the gods in their temples.

The Sumerians were definitely the most sophisticated and cultured of their time, with painters, sculptors, artists and musicians and with a reputation for astronomy, medicine, mathematics and philosophy. They were adept at weaving, leatherwork and metal work. They painted pottery and carved sculptures. Using bronze, they made knives, daggers and spears. They developed the cuneiform script with hieroglyph pictures on clay tablets. They codified the law, kept records of transactions and debts and even set up courts for trials. They domesticated sheep, pigs, goats, donkeys, oxen and horses, using the latter for transport, ploughing and harrowing.

The state of Sumer recorded its first war against the Elamites in Northern Iran. This was to be the forerunner of numerous wars and battles fought in the Middle East, which sadly continues to this day. Clearly, competition for land, power or religious beliefs seem to be a feature of human behaviour.

However, the population in Sumer declined as the land became less fertile, fused with salts which some plants could not tolerate.

Akkadia

One of Sumer's city states called Akkad became the centre of Akkadia, although its actual location is not known. It was headed by King Sargon, allegedly a foundling like Romulus, put in a basket on the river by his priestess mother and found by a shepherd. When he too became King in 2334 BC he launched a campaign that united all the states of Sumer and Akkadia and within a decade had extended his conquests from the Persian Gulf to the Mediterranean and up to the Taurus mountains in Turkey.

It is believed that Akkadia had the first known army of professional soldiers which each of the city states had to provide. Constant strife and warfare led to the development of helmeted warriors armed with spears, leading an infantry phalanx six files deep, as in later Greece. Thus armed, King Sargon led his troops on a chariot, drawn by four wild asses, followed by spearmen, bowmen and archers. The King, now known as Sargon the Great, led his army in thirty-four battles and never lost one. He carried on fighting until he died aged 55, in 2279 BC. Thereafter, the Akkadian Empire, as it was known, only lasted for another 180 years, although Sumer itself survived as a State.

Ancient Egypt

Hunter-gatherers have been living along the Nile for 120,000 years. But they did not start serious agriculture and animal husbandry until about 5500 BC, using oxen for ploughing like the Sumerians. The people were able to make tools and decorate pottery with ceramic glaze. They traded with their neighbours around the Mediterranean, importing obsidian from Ethiopia, and exporting copper, gold and semi-precious stones. However, the beginnings of their empire did not really begin until the upper and lower reaches of the Nile were merged by King Menes in 3100 BC.

The Kings or Pharaohs had total control, but the Queen too had an official role. One, Queen Hatshepsut, was actually crowned as King. The country was divided into forty-two regions under the control of a nomarch, and a top-heavy administration kept tight control. The nomarch oversaw the storage of grain and special metals. Prices were fixed for grain, clothing and cattle. The labourers were paid in grain, not money, and are they are known to have gone on strike when they were not paid!

From 2686 BC they had established a justice system with some fierce punishments, ranging from beatings to decapitation, drowning and impaling on stakes! Court cases were decided by councils of elders. The Egyptians were great builders, erecting hundreds of pyramids, temples and obelisks, although labourers only lived in mud-brick and timber houses. They were also skilled boat builders, constructing planked boats as early as 3000 BC, that sailed along the Nile, using the wind one way and the stream the other.

Social status was stratified with nobles and the state owning much of the land. Men and women had equal status, and slaves even had their own rights. Their diet was fairly basic, bread, beer, onions and garlic, with some meat, fish and fruit. Daily activities included wrestling, hunting and playing music, with several different instruments used in their social and religious ceremonies.

Writing was common from 3000 BC, using hieroglyphs that read right to left. They were skilled in mathematics, medicine and technology and they were also experts in irrigation. For example, the pharaoh Senusret III and his son organised the construction of a huge channel from the River Nile to the swamp at Fayum Valley, which created a lake of six billion cubic metres, bigger than any reservoir we have since created. This provided water for agriculture and prevented any serious drought.

Although Egypt had a strong military, the Hyksos people from the Delta seized control of the country in 1785 BC and were only defeated by Ahmose I after thirty years. Life for the next thousand years was fairly peaceful under the pharaohs, but Egypt's power gradually declined and it was taken over, first by the Assyrians, followed by the Persians, then by Alexander the Great in 332 BC, and finally by the Romans.

The Indus Valley

The third most important civilisation alongside Sumer and Egypt, covering much of North East India and Pakistan, centred on the River Indus and its alluvial plain. The Indus people farmed and herded cattle from 7000 BC but it was not until 3500 BC that thousands of settlements were established. The people had mudbrick houses with open-roof kitchens and inner courtyards which had good water facilities, drainage and sewerage. The streets were set out in a grid system, packed with traders and artisans, just like today. They were noted for their mathematical skills and developed the first system of weights and measures. The people all had equal status, with no dominant ruler, only city authorities. They were noted for bronze, stone and terracotta *figure*s, and necklaces and bangles which they traded overseas.

However, like the Sumerian and Egyptian civilisations, the population declined after a series of earthquakes, weaker monsoons and droughts, the impacts of which they were unable to mitigate without the Egyptians' irrigation skills.

Babylon

There was a small town in Akkadia called Babylon, which grew into a city of 2000 people. From 1792 BC the Amorite ruler, King Hammurabi freed Babylon from control by Elam, allegedly with a standing army of only 5600 spearmen, bowman, archers and charioteers. The King then conquered many of the cities in Mesopotamia and invaded what was Jordan and Syria. He turned Babylon into a holy city and cultural centre, with a deserved reputation for medicine, mathematics, astronomy and philosophy. The King ran an efficient bureaucracy and promulgated the Babylon law code.

The empire declined after the King's death and was sacked by the Hittites in 1595 BC. But Babylon remained as a kingdom and an important cultural and religious centre, despite coming under a number of different rulers, until it was finally conquered by Alexander the Great in 323 BC.

The Assyrian/Akkadian Empire

Assyria was the world's longest lasting empire. It was quite unique in that it had three separate periods of imperial domination over 1800 years, right up to 609 BC. Its people were originally a mixture of Akkadians and Sumerians. They were involved in many of the wars and alliances round Mesopotamia. Males were conscripted into military service, either defending their territory or invading their neighbours. From 2500 BC the country was led by pastoral king-priests, with an elaborate social and legal system, worshipping their main god Assur. Authority was exercised by an assembly of elders operating out of the capital. For a short time, Assyria was absorbed into the Akkadian empire under King Sargon but became independent again in 2100 BC.

The Amorite dynasty took over in 1754 BC and within thirty years the empire achieved its peak with control over most of the Middle East, from Egypt to Persia and from the Persian

Gulf to Turkey and the Caucasus. The Assyrians had a strong merchant class which traded metals round their known world, including gold, silver, copper and iron. Their architecture developed a unique style with palaces sporting colourful wall decorations. Most of the people were bilingual, speaking Sumerian and Akkadian, and they continued to use the cuneiform script, writing with a reed stylus on clay tablets.

From 1450 BC Assyria was dominated by the Mitanni and became a vassal state, but once again broke free and became independent in 1362 BC. Thereafter there was a revival under King Eriba-Adad I and his dynasty, taking over what are now parts of Syria, Iran and Turkey.

Once again, the country went into decline in 1050 BC. However, it rose again under successive dynasties from 910 BC to become a vast nation, stretching from Egypt to Persia and dominating the whole of the Middle East. This too did not last, and by 609 BC, with the fall of Harran, the Assyrian Empire was destroyed as a political entity and just became a provincial province.

The Persian Empire

Nomadic people from Central Asia settled in the region of Persia alongside the Gulf in the seventh century BC, where King Cyrus, called Cyrus the Great, threw off Assyrian rule, established the first Persian Empire in 550 BC and conquered the Medes, Babylon and Lydia. Cyrus died in 530 BC. He was succeeded by his son and then, after some family infighting, was succeeded by his grandson Darius I.

Both Cyrus and Darius were clever and strong military leaders, achieving extraordinary expansion of their territory and raising a relatively small Achaemenid tribe to a world power in thirty years. This stretched from Macedonia and Thrace, across most of Turkey, Bulgaria, Romania, Ukraine and part of Russia, right up to the Indus Valley and covered the whole of the Levant, Egypt and part of Arabia.

Both leaders allowed religious freedom. Darius introduced a monetary and tax system and built many large-scale temples and palaces, using craftsmen, stone cutters, metalworkers and goldsmiths drawn from all over the empire. The youth of his day were all taught to ride, box, draw and speak the truth. To lie was a cardinal sin, even in some cases punishable by death.

Both Cyrus and Darius allowed each region some autonomy under a satrap or governor. They even allowed satrapies to retain their own kings, laws, language and customs. Although the size of the empire was vast, Darius linked the regions with highways and even the furthest frontiers could be reached in fifteen days by Persian couriers from Persepolis, the capital.

Cyrus built up a professional army, drawing troops from conquered countries, whilst Darius built their first navy, using Greeks, Egyptians and Phoenicians to man them. Powered by sail and manpower, their ships could hold up to 300 troops. Their armies had both infantry and cavalry, with horses protected by armour, and also included elephants.

After Darius died it was clearly difficult to control the largest empire of its time and several rebellions broke out. His son Xerxes I managed to retain control for a time. But, after he died, weakened by the satrapies' fighting amongst themselves, central control gradually broke down over the next hundred years, and were easy pickings for the Greeks. They were defeated by Alexander the Great between 334 and 331 BC.

What was Persia's legacy? Apart from the Persians' legendary warfare, they had an efficient administration, legal and tax system. They introduced gold and silver coins. Their system of government, which allowed satrapies to retain their own language, customs, religion and kings, was duly copied by the Romans and later empires.

The Chinese Empire

Although the earliest written records only date from 1250 BC, the history of the Chinese Empire prior to that time has since been written up. We know that the rich agricultural areas along the Yangtze and Yellow Rivers were on a par with those of Mesopotamia and the Indus Valley. Rice was cultivated there in 8000BC and millet shortly afterwards. Cliff carvings of that time have been found, with pictographs showing the sun, the moon and the gods. There is evidence of bronze materials, pottery and jewellery. You can also see the 8000 Terracotta Warriors in Lanzhou, dating from 2021 BC, with plaster casts of infantry, cavalrymen, archers and different ranks of officers. We also know of their sophisticated irrigation systems with underground channels carrying water from the mountains to the fields, still used today.

The Xia dynasty, starting in 2070 BC was the first imperial dynasty. It was followed over the next four thousand years up to AD 1912, by a number of other dynasties, named Shang, Zhou, Quin, Han, Xia, Jim, Su, Tang, Song, Yuan, Ming and Qing.

The Zhou dynasty, 1046 – 256 BC was the longest lasting. Theirs was a feudal and elitist society, with royal ranking up to emperor, and a strong military needed to control the warring states. They operated under what they called 'The Mandate of Heaven' which provided a religious compact between the Zhou people and the sky gods, asserting their moral authority and entitling them to take over all the Shang wealth and territories. In return the rulers had to uphold the principles of harmony and honour, failing which they could be replaced. Confucius, born in 551 BC, notably taught all his students to observe personal morality, justice, kindness and sincerity, strong family worship and ancestor veneration. His teachings, secular not religious, are still important in China today, alongside Buddhism and Taoist beliefs.

The Han dynasty, 202 BC to AD 220, was a golden age for China, opening up the Silk Road and developing international trade. The emperor was the supreme judge, lawgiver and commander-in-chief, receiving nobles and ambassadors in the imperial palace. He had supporting ministers, including a Chancellor who managed the budget. News from each of his provinces was sent to the emperor by mounted couriers who could ride 400 kilometres at one stretch, changing horses en route. Conscription for all males was at the age of 23 when they were directed into the infantry, cavalry or navy. Property and poll taxes were paid by all the people, even peasants, often oppressed by their landlords. Large agricultural estates and mines were held by wealthy nobles who sponsored new forms of mechanical tools. Bronze and iron were used for weapons, tools, ploughshares and domestic utensils. Emperor Qu nationalised the highly profitable iron, salt and liquor industries, whilst the whole economy thrived.

However, the dynasty became very unstable in the 180's BC with rebellions, military plots and family conflict. After thirty-five years, Emperor Xian relinquished control, and the Han dynasty ended.

During the time of the Tang dynasty, AD 618 – 907, with its capital at Jian in central China, the population grew up to 80 million. In the census of AD 754, there were 1859 cities, 321 prefectures and 1538 counties throughout the empire – far superior to Europe at the time. There were also thousands of expatriate merchants living alongside the Chinese in their cities. The Tang territory reached their farthest point - from, what are now, Vietnam to Korea, and north of Kashmir to the China Sea, with several countries paying tribute. It is thought that China reached its cultural peak during the Tang dynasty, particularly in literature, poetry and art. The legal code was established and examinations were held for all bureaucratic positions. They were advanced in medicine, astrology, woodblock printing and cartography. Everyone had to pay poll taxes and property taxes in order to support a large army of 500,000 troops, but hard-pressed peasants were excused from paying if they enlisted in the army. Social rights for women, whether lowly weavers or high placed courtesans, were more liberal than elsewhere, and we have pictures of courtesans playing polo.

The Song dynasty which followed, from 960 – 1279, was split into two dynasties, North and South. It is believed to have been the most advanced economy in the mediaeval period. It had fleets trading all around the known world. It had investments in joint stock companies and Guilds for artisans which controlled training, wages, taxes and prices. The Song society was well governed, with all civil servants required to sit competitive examinations. Their military is said to have had one million soldiers at its height, divided into battalions, companies and platoons. Their cavalry used halberds, swords, bows, spears and fire lances containing shrapnel and gunpowder, which they had invented. In the navy, their ships could hold thousands of troops. They smelted iron and copper, using coal not charcoal, for making arms and utensils. They issued six billion copper coins as well as paper banknotes.

Social life was vibrant. There were special entertainment quarters with banquets, festivals, music, performing arts and storytellers, together with thousands of individual clubs. At home, people played Go and other board games. Clothing depended on social status - hemp, cotton or skins in black or white for the poor, and silks with gold ornaments and precious stones for the rich. Food for the poor was basic - rice, pork and fish. But recorded meal menus for the rich have featured all kinds of animals, fruits and vegetables.

However, the Northern dynasty only lasted until 1234 and was taken over, first by the Jin dynasty, and then by the Mongolian empire. The Southern dynasty carried on until 1279 when one of Genghis Khan's successors, Kublai Khan, took over and renamed it the Yuan dynasty. This too did not last very long, only ninety-seven years, with much discontent. After a series of floods, drought and famine, the dynasty was decisively beaten by the Ming.

The Ming dynasty, 1368-1644, was characterised by its concentration on agriculture, the growth of private industry and more urbanisation. With a standing army of one million, they occupied Vietnam and helped to push the Japanese out of Korea, which was a tribute state. But then they became more isolationist. With weakening control in Manchuria, the local tribes broke away, forming their own Qing state.

Over several decades, the Qing state conquered the Ming people, at a cost of twenty-five million lives, and founded their own dynasty. Taking over Taiwan and advancing into Central Asia, the Qing dynasty reached its zenith in 1796, having the world's largest economy and one-third of the world population.

However, in the nineteenth century their power declined as they suffered in the Opium Wars, the Japanese War and a series of rebellions and clan wars. Finally, in 1911, a military uprising sealed their fate and a republic was declared the following year.

The Greek/Seleucid Empire

Emerging from the Dark Ages, Greece was split into tribal areas in the sixth century BC with four independent cities, Athens, Sparta, Corinth and Thebes. There was continued strife amongst the city states, particularly between Athens and Sparta, who engaged in a series of Peloponnesian Wars between 431 and 404 BC, and again between 395 and 387 BC. These wars were periodically halted by peace treaties, which were immediately broken.

Finally, Philip II restored peace and unified the kingdom. Philip then engaged in another war with Persia, helped by his son Alexander. But he was assassinated in 336 BC and local rebellions broke out which Alexander had to quell. Meanwhile the population of Greece had grown to over ten million. And, with all the disturbances at home, many Greeks emigrated to all over the Mediterranean, even to Pakistan and Afghanistan, where they set up local settlements.

Alexander, then only 20, engaged in a whole series of campaigns overseas, conquering Egypt, Mesopotamia, Syria, Turkey, Persia, Afghanistan and Pakistan, and building up an empire as big as those of Cyrus and Darius. He carried on into India, but his troops were tired of warfare. He had to turn back, never having lost a battle in thirteen years. Even so, there were vast territories to control and Alexander gave each colony semi-autonomy, with just three power bases in Egypt, Macedonia and Seleucid.

Sadly, at the early age of 33, Alexander died, allegedly of a fever, but he may have been poisoned. However, he left a legacy of a strong and cultured society, noted for literature, poetry, politics, philosophy, science, mathematics and medicine. Great names of the past, Plato, Socrates, Homer and Hippocrates testify to the founding of a modern democracy, whose influence spread over the rest of the world.

What of Alexander's own legacy? He was obviously an outstanding general with both tactical and logistical skills. When he had a standing army of about 65,000, he would have had to provide 200,00 pounds of grain and double that amount of water each week to feed his troops. By requiring each of his soldiers to carry their own food and equipment, he created the most mobile and fastest moving army the world had ever seen. In this respect he was helped by his father's own dictate, which had abolished camp followers.

After Alexander died, the empire was split into several kingdoms controlled by his generals. Seleucus, one of Alexander's cavalry commanders, was awarded Babylonia in 321 BC which he then used as a base to build up a new empire, including Mesopotamia, Armenia, Anatolia, Syria, Cappadocia and Parthia. But, after Seleucus died, his successors struggled to hold on to their territories. Faced by Greece, Egypt and the new newly emerging Roman Empire, the short-lived Seleucid empire collapsed.

Roman Empire

Starting off with the beginning of Rome, it is alleged that King Amulius ordered the two grandchildren of King Numitor, Romulus and Remus, to be drowned in case they threatened his rule, but the servant put them in a basket, which eventually floated to a bank where they were suckled by a she-wolf and picked up by a shepherd who brought them up. When they later found out the truth, they killed Amulius and took over the throne. But, after a series of arguments, Romulus killed Remus. During his reign, Romulus proclaimed himself King and established a senate of upper-class men, notable for wearing a flash of purple on their togas. For the next 200 years there was a series of kings - up to 590 BC when, after a rebellion against King Tarquin, Rome was declared a republic, controlled by two consuls.

From then on, first Rome, then Italy, were involved in an incredibly long series of wars, both on land and at sea, starting against the Sabines, the Etruscans, the Samnites, the Gauls and the King of Epirus, right up to 275 BC. Then followed the three Punic wars against Carthage in which Hannibal famously took his troops across the Alps with elephants all the way to the gates of Rome, but was ultimately beaten back, and Carthage was then destroyed.

Wars with Sparta and Macedonia followed, but Italy was still not yet a big power. Only when the Seleucid Wars of 192-183 BC finished with a clear Roman victory did Rome extend its territory, taking over the Greek states and Asia minor. In 113 BC, the republic was involved in wars against the Celtic and German tribes but both sides suffered heavy losses, leading to political upheaval in Rome. It took fifty different wars between 500 BC and 31 BC for the republic to control the whole of western Europe, north Africa, Egypt and the Middle East. But its peak was reached under Trajan in AD 117, when the republic contained 70 million people, one fifth of the world's population.

Following the example of Cyrus, Darius and Alexander, the republic allowed the conquered territories a degree of autonomy. However, each was controlled by a powerful provincial government that handled the administration, collected taxes, and reported back to the emperor and his legates. Each province had to provide troops for the Roman army, war captives for slaves and hostages to ensure good behaviour. All Rome wanted was booty, a supply of grain, a supply of slaves and the provinces' obedience. Most of the provincials were expected to speak Latin, which had overtaken Greek, but local languages like Coptic in Egypt were accepted.

The Roman army reached a size of twenty-eight legions, each of 4000 to 5000, making a total of 150,000 men. Soldiers signed on for twenty years, and then five years as reserves. There were ten cohorts to one legion and six centuries to one cohort. The infantry formed a wide phalanx of twenty men, well-spaced and six deep, each using swords rather than spears. The Romans were the first to use heavy cavalry with javelins, using the infantry as a central anchor. To help control their empire, they built 240,000 miles of roads and were able to reach distant parts relatively quickly.

Citizens were registered by class. Patricians had a better chance of advancement, but Plebeians, whether craftsmen, soldiers or farmers, through political or military service or else personal fortune, could rise up the ladder. Families were controlled by their fathers, but women had more freedom than in other empires and could own property. Only the slaves, whose average mortality rate was shockingly below the age of 20, had a worse outlook, although they could buy or be given their freedom and become citizens.

Private education was only for the rich, either in schools which were introduced in 250 BC, or with a tutor. Parents were expected to teach their children to grow up as model citizens. Boys reached adulthood as early as age 14. Literacy was still at a relatively low level, but to keep up with the paperwork you could always use a scribe!

With all its splendid military, cultural and artistic achievements, the empire could not continue for ever and it started to decline in AD 180. The whole of the third century AD was notable for invasions, plagues, civil strife and social disorder. Emperor Diocletian did manage to restore order and split the empire into four regions, each ruled as a separate empire, but that too collapsed until Constantine the Great established Constantinople as the new capital of the Eastern Empire. The Western Empire officially ended when Emperor Romulus Augustus abdicated in AD 476, giving up the Eastern Empire, later to be called the Byzantine Empire, which carried on for another thousand years.

Byzantine Empire

In AD 330, Constantine moved the seat of the Eastern Roman Empire to Constantinople. Following his conversion, Christianity became the preferred religion, although other religions were tolerated. Part of the Western Roman Empire was retained, but after Constantine died the Balkans were lost to the Slavs, and Egypt fell to the Persians.

In AD 867, Basil I ascended to the throne, beginning the Macedonian dynasty. After a series of wars fought by his successors, the empire once again expanded, stretching from Calabria in Italy to Armenia, and from Syria to the Danube. The conversion of Bulgarians, Serbs and Russians to orthodox Christianity re-drew the religious map of Europe.

During the Komnenian dynasty, Constantinople remained the leading city of the Christian world in terms of size, wealth, trade and culture. However, the crusaders attacked in AD 1203 and the empire was split up once again into Nicaea, Epirus and Trebizond. Over a long civil war, most of the empire was overrun. Finally, Constantinople was taken over by the Ottomans under Sultan Mehmed II in 1453.

The Ottoman Empire

The Ottomans originated in Turkey under Osman II, a tribal leader. His successors took over the Balkans, Anatolia and Constantinople, and then gradually expanded into Persia, Hungary, Mesopotamia and Egypt, becoming the dominant naval force controlling the Mediterranean. By 1556 the Balkans, Greece and North Africa were under Ottoman control.

However, the Ottomans eventually came up against the Spanish, Serbs, Hapsburgs and Russians, losing all their North African territories, whilst Bulgaria, Romania, Serbia and Montenegro all gained their independence. Finally, as recently as a hundred years ago, after the Turkish War of Independence, the republic of Turkey was established in its place, and the empire was finished.

The Habsburg Empire

The Habsburg Empire is included here, not because of the conquest of territories but because it was a central European monarchy that ruled over much of Europe from the thirteenth to the twentieth century by virtue of family inter-marriages. Over 650 years, the Habsburg family accumulated many inheritances, titles and possessions, including Austria, Bavaria, Vienna, Bohemia, Moravia, Czech Republic, south west Poland, Hungary, Slovakia, Romania and parts of Yugoslavia - including the Spanish Kings, who ruled over their own empire from 1516 to 1700. The Habsburgs were also head of a different non-territorial empire, the Holy Roman Empire, between 1438 and 1806.

Their journey began with the election of Rudolph I as King of the Germans in 1273, who then conquered Austria to give to his son. The monarchy acquired the Netherlands by marriage and then began a quite extraordinary mixture of family holdings and alliances spread over Europe.

At the time parts of Europe were split up into what I call a 'dynastic melange'. In Germany, for example, right up to the nineteenth century there were 1320 independent kingdoms, dukedoms, duchies, archbishoprics, principalities and cities, until they were taken over and consolidated by the Prussians in 1848-52.

Both Joseph II and his mother, Empress Maria Theresa, attempted to consolidate the Habsburgs' rule, but it never became a cohesive empire and collapsed at the end of the First World War.

The Spanish Empire

Although not much talked about, the growth and subsequent decline of the Spanish Empire, with its numerous wars, is perhaps more interesting than the British Empire and its legacy is not fully appreciated. In a treaty in 1493, Castile and Portugal divided the world into two spheres, giving Asia and Africa to Portugal and the western hemisphere to Castile. Despite the treaty, Castile took over coastal towns in North Africa, and then took over the Canary Islands.

The Crown of Castile gave Columbus widespread powers to explore, settle and control new territories in the 1490's. This started the process of colonisation, firstly with Hispaniola, Jamaica, Cuba and Puerto Rico in the Caribbean. This was followed up by tiny armies of conquistadores attacking the Aztecs, and then the Incas, to get control of Peru and large parts of South America. Spurred on by shipments of gold and silver brought back to Cadiz, helped by smallpox and other diseases wiping out the local indigenous population, Castile's tentacles spread over the whole of South America, apart from Brazil, which was retained by Portugal. Castile then moved into central America, taking over Panama, Nicaragua and Mexico, moving east into Spanish Florida and north into Canada. Then, in 1516, Charles I of Castile inherited Aragon's possessions from Ferdinand I under the Habsburgs, thus uniting Spain for the first time.

By that time, Charles I was the most powerful monarch in Europe, abdicating to his son Philip II in 1558. Philip fought a series of wars against France, Italy, Germany and even the Ottomans in eastern Europe. He could also have invaded England had the Armada not failed in 1588. The Spanish Empire achieved its peak in 1580 when Philip claimed the Portuguese Empire and controlled most of the trading ports in the new world.

However, the cost of fighting wars and illegal smuggling, which syphoned off shipments of silver, depleted the Spanish Treasury. Spain was declared bankrupt and Philip was forced to sign peace treaties with his neighbours. Nonetheless, trading continued unabated, not only in Mexico and South America but also in Asia where Castile had been given jurisdiction over the Philippines.

The empire then began a slow decline. In 1581 part of the Netherlands achieved independence. In 1640 the Portuguese rebelled against the Spanish, and eight years later Spain recognised its independence. In the Caribbean, Spain's claims for territory were disputed by the English, French and Dutch. After the death of Charles II, who was childless, the Spanish crown was contested in the War of Spanish Succession in 1713. Philip V became King and ceded the Spanish Netherlands, Naples and Milan to Austria and Savoy. England picked up Menorca and Gibraltar but this still left Spain with the Americas, Philippines and part of North Africa.

The rest of the eighteenth century was both more peaceful and more prosperous as silver production tripled and shipping greatly expanded - but the tide turned in the nineteenth century. In the secret treaty of San Ildefonso in 1800, Spain exchanged the vast territory of Louisiana, stretching right up to Canada, which France had previously ceded to Spain in 1765, for just the province of Tuscany. In the Napoleonic War, Spain was defeated by Napoleon who put his brother Joseph on the throne. In South America, the local juntas became more rebellious and from 1810 to 1833 all the South American colonies and Mexico became independent. Finally, in the six-month Spanish American War in 1898, the United States took over Cuba and Puerto Rico, and paid $20 million for the purchase of the Philippines.

So, what was the legacy of Spain's empire? Whilst their conquistadores in the 1500's were rapacious soldiers of fortune and Spain was constantly at war, Spain can claim that they opened up new trade routes, installed governance in new territories, founded hundreds of new towns and cities, built ports, roads and canals, spread the Catholic faith, built cathedrals, notable colonial residences, hospitals and schools, and developed modern agriculture and husbandry. The oldest universities were founded by Spanish scholars and Catholic missionaries. The Spanish dollar became the first global currency, and now the Spanish language is spoken by 470 million people worldwide.

The Russian Empire

Tsar Ivan III laid the foundations for the growth of the empire, tripling its size between 1463 and 1503, taking over territories by conquest, purchase or marriage contract. He defeated the republic of Novgorod in 1471 and took over the principalities of Yaroslavl, Rostov, Tver and Vyatka. Lithuania was then ceded to Russia in 1503.

The next biggest change came under Peter the Great, who expanded the Tsardom into a major European power. Tall, at six foot eight, he first travelled round Europe to see how it operated. He returned to replace the social system and set up a Senate in place of the old Boyar Council. He changed the calendar, enforced children's education, stopped arranged marriages, and hired foreign architects to design palatial buildings. His first military task was to secure a Baltic enclave which was achieved by war with Sweden, when he first occupied, and then secured provinces south of Finland. In the Great Northern War, he took over Latvia and Estonia. The following year, attacking a weakened Persia, he advanced into the Caucasus. In 1721 he declared the Tsardom an empire, which lasted under the Romanovs and their matrilineal German branch right up to 1917.

His grandson, Peter III only reigned for six months before he was dethroned and possibly murdered. However, he achieved miracles in his short reign. He passed 220 laws. He promulgated religious freedom. He abolished the secret police and exempted the nobles from military service. The circumstances of his death are not properly known. But it is clear that his wife benefited most.

Peter had married a German princess, Catherine, who became Empress herself from 1762 – 1796. With her successful generals and victories over the Ottomans, she crushed the Crimean Khanate, colonised the areas surrounding the Black Sea, partitioned the Polish-Lithuanian Commonwealth and colonised Alaska. She modernised Russia along the same lines as Peter the Great, reformed the administration, founded many towns and cities and was a fervent patron of the arts.

Soon after Catherine's reign, Napoleon attacked Russia, his army nearly reaching Moscow but, like Hitler later, was forced by the brutal Russian winter and shortage of supplies to retreat. In the following years, up to 1850, the country lagged behind the rest of Europe. Educational standards and literacy were low, agricultural productivity on the large estates managed by serfs was also very poor and the economy faltered. Furthermore, the country was in a continual financial crisis, unable to support the economy. At the time, the army took nearly half of Russia's taxable income and the administration and the upkeep of the Imperial Court at St. Petersburg took another twenty per cent. Then, in 1854/55, the Russians were defeated by Britain, France and Turkey in the Crimean War.

Alexander II ascended the throne in 1855 as Emperor of Russia, King of Poland and Grand Duke of Finland. He did undertake a number of reforms, including the emancipation of the serfs in 1861. However, the serfs were given an inadequate allocation of land to feed their families, they now had to pay taxes, and they were worse off than before, whilst the nobles still held onto much of the land. Alexander did re-organise the judicial system. He abolished corporal punishment, promoted local self-government and university education, imposed universal military service, and removed some of the nobles' privileges. He fought a brief war with the Ottomans, pushed Russian territory into Siberia and conquered Turkestan, but sold Alaska in 1867.

Unfortunately, he was assassinated in 1881 and followed by a reactionary, Alexander III, who made little impact and died in 1894.

Meanwhile, Russia's population was growing apace. With only 14 million people in 1722, it had risen to 150 million by 1891. Nicholas II came to the throne as the economy started to recover, particularly in heavy industry. The mines flourished with rising production of iron, copper, zinc, precious metals, coal and petroleum, and much of industry was being updated with European machinery. Production of coal tripled in the 1890's and iron ore doubled. Both grain and beet production also increased. Transportation improved with new railways laid down by the army, covering vast distances to the east.

During Nicholas' reign, the political split between left and right widened, the army suffered multiple defeats in the war against Japan, the soldiers were disaffected and the workers complained about low wages. There were 176 strikes between 1895 and 1905. Riots broke out in 1905 with mutiny on the battleship Potemkin. Nicholas formed the first Duma, the lower parliamentary house, but unwisely clung on to supreme power. Three more Dumas followed but the unrest continued and Russia's entry into the first world war proved unsuccessful. There were two revolutions in February and March 1917 and Nicholas abdicated, thus ending the empire.

At its peak, in 1914, the empire was one of the world's largest, stretching across most of Ukraine, Poland, Finland, Belarus, Azerbaijan, Armenia, Georgia and the Caucasus. Even today it still covers vast territory, and just like the Tsars, exercises firm control over the population.

The British Empire

Finally, we come to the British Empire, which by 1913 ended up with a population of 412 million, 23 per cent of the world population. But it was not a unified structure, more a patchwork of countries brought together under different circumstances. Although Britain was involved in a number of wars, there was never an emperor like Alexander or Sargon the Great attacking his neighbours or seeking warlike conquests. Instead there was a miscellany of accretions to the empire over 300 years, through the discovery of new lands, protection of settlements and ports, escape from religious persecution in Britain, pursuance of missionary zeal, the lure of free farmland, and sadly the transport of slaves. It was also influenced by the loss of thirteen American colonies, which forced Britain to look elsewhere.

Actually, the first attempt to settle overseas in Newfoundland and Carolina failed in 1583/84, as did attempts to settle in Grenada and St. Lucia in 1604 to 1609. However, they did succeed in St. Kitts, Barbados and Nevis in 1624 to 1629 and provided Britain with valuable sugar. In 1665 Britain annexed Jamaica from the Spanish and colonised the Bahamas in the following year, but these were relatively minor developments.

In terms of size and population, the development of the Raj in India was the most significant. It was started by a private joint stock company, set up for trade, called the East India Company in 1600. The Company first set up factories on the east coast. In this case, there were a number of minor wars against the Nizam of Hyderabad, fought by Company troops between 1757 and 1818, and against the Sikhs in 1845/9. The Company annexed a whole series of states, signing treaties or alliances with the ruling princes, nawabs and maharajas. The Company only ceded control when the British Government established the British Raj in 1858 under a governor-general.

In America, Britain was beaten in the War of Independence and a republic was declared in 1776. North of the border, France claimed possession in 1534, calling it New France, but

Britain claimed Newfoundland as a colony in 1583. A census there in 1665 showed that British settlers vastly outnumbered the French, who only had 3,215 inhabitants. A century later, France ceded the territory to Britain.

In Australia, James Cook claimed the East Coast in 1770 and in 1788 a fleet of British ships arrived at Botany Bay in New South Wales with a cargo of convicts, as well as some free settlers. Between 1788 and 1868 over 160,000 convicts were transported there. Australia was then divided in half. The East was put under the administration of a governor in Sydney, and the western half was called New Holland. In 1836 a new colony, Southern Australia, was created in between the two. The news in 1831 that gold had been found there spurred on a wave of immigrants from Britain and Ireland, boosting the population. New South Wales was the first state to get autonomous government in 1855, followed by Victoria, Tasmania and South Australia, although Western Australia did not achieve autonomy until 1890. The Commonwealth of Australia was established on January 1st, 1901.

Across the water, New Zealand was discovered by Cook in 1769 and over three voyages he circumnavigated and mapped the island. From the 1790's whaling ships started trading with the Maoris. In 1817 the governor of New South Wales was given legal authority over New Zealand. In 1834, hearing that the New Zealand Company planned to buy up large tracts of land there, the British Government stepped in and sent out a governor to get the Maoris to cede their sovereignty; and self-government was achieved in 1846.

The final bit of the imperial jigsaw was in Africa. Cecil Rhodes, a mining magnate, head of De Beers and former prime minister of Cape Colony, obtained a charter from the government for his company, British South Africa Company, to rule and make concessions and treaties in an area from the Limpopo River to the Great Lakes. The company officially took control over Rhodesia and Nyasaland between 1895 and 1898. Kenya became a British protectorate after the Anglo-German Agreement in 1890 and Uganda became a protectorate the same year. In the west, the Royal Nigeria Company had a trade charter from the government, but this was revoked in 1899 and southern Nigeria was created a protectorate in 1900, adding the Lagos colony in 1906 and Northern Nigeria in 1914.

In South Africa the Cape, controlled by the Dutch, was invaded by, and ceded to Britain in 1814. Natal was proclaimed a colony in 1843 after Britain annexed the Boer republic of Natalia, but the Orange Free State and Transvaal were only transferred to Britain in 1902 after the Boers were defeated in the Boer War. The Union of South Africa was made a self-governing dominion of the British Empire in 1909.

The Second World War drew the dominions and colonies together to fight Nazi Germany but, thereafter, the 'winds of change' finally blew the empire away. By 1965 it had fallen to a population of only 5 million, the majority of those in Hong Kong.

So, what of Britain's legacy? It is now fashionable to trash its legacy as rapacious, tainted by slave trading, but I think it can at least state a claim for parliamentary democracy, sound colonial government, a fine legal system, the spread of the English language and the introduction of a number of new sports!

Having looked at all the principal empires from Sumer up to now, one lesson stands out. NO empire lasts for ever!

CHAPTER 6

THE NEXT HUNDRED YEARS

Whilst the future looms forward into infinity, I have tried to narrow down the timescale into four segments of a hundred, a thousand, one million years and over one million years. Sadly, I don't have the prophetic vision of H G Wells, whose writing included science fiction and foresaw the advent of television, aircraft, and space travel, but I am open to conjecture from anyone with his vision.

To start with, I have looked back a hundred years to the 'swinging 1920's' to see what changes there have been since then. First, look back to your own parents, grandparents and their parents' lives to see how they were living and what has changed. For my part, life is not much different from theirs - similar diet, health and social activities. But there are now washing machines, better cars, and air-flights, better communication and television. So, what were the main changes over this period? -

Obviously, smart phones and other communication systems, computers, artificial intelligence, social media, television and different transport have changed our lives. Looking at the world as a whole, the population has risen from 2 billion in 1920 to 7.8 billion in 2020, a massive increase. The change in crude birth and death rates per 1000 is also remarkable, even from 1950 as we can see below:

DATE	BIRTH RATE	DEATH RATE	POPULATION
1950	36.9	19.1	2.5 billion
2020	17.5	8.1	7.8 billion
forecast 2050	14.6	9.7	9.4 billion

In 2004 the UN Population Division projected that the population would peak at 9.2 billion in 2075. Then they realised that they had underestimated the birth rate in Africa and in 2014 they raised their projection to 10.9 billion in 2100, rising slowly thereafter. Some biologists have projected much higher *figure*s, even as high as 15 billion, which would seriously affect both livelihoods and resources, bringing Malthus theory into play, but I am confident that the world population will be much lower. For one thing, women are marrying later, restricting the size of their families, either through contraception, shortage of funds or the need for a better lifestyle for their children.

At the moment, half the world's population live in countries with fertility rates below replacement levels, so we should carefully watch future levels, particularly in India, China and Africa.

Looking at the economies in different countries, some have done better than others, particularly China which has become a super power and is pushing ahead with 'Belt and Road plans' to extend its power worldwide. But overall, poverty has declined, education and living standards have improved, and democracy has survived, even if only by a bare margin in some countries. Racial, gender and social equality have improved, and there is generally more tolerance, even if religious divisions still create unnecessary conflict. Looking at the material world, technology has advanced apace, particularly in nuclear power, the use of robots in manufacturing and, of course, communication systems.

In the next hundred years, changes are likely to speed up, although economic standards may only improve by 2 or 3 per cent, per year, with dips every time there is a serious epidemic or financial crash. Poverty will hopefully be alleviated and living standards should improve, providing the increase in gross international product is not eaten up by excessive population growth. Social, racial and gender equality should improve further, but intolerance between religions could still lead to international strife. Housing standards, still appalling in some countries, should improve, using modular construction, with better water, sewerage, schools and hospitals. Personal health may improve, due to medical advances, but there is still a serious risk of increased obesity and diabetes. Life expectancy should improve, although the rate of growth has almost come to a halt in advanced economies. Some people forecast that we will live to 120 and beyond. The oldest Frenchwoman did live to be 122, but no-one has matched that recently. In 2004 the UN forecast that average global life expectancy would rise to 97 by 2100 and 106 by 2300. But, despite human desire to live longer, I believe this is overoptimistic.

The forecast that dead people could be revived with their brains intact, when medical knowledge is improved, if they are first immersed in liquid nitrogen is, I believe, fanciful, at least in the next hundred years! There is no doubt that modern medical treatments will keep people alive longer, but with cancer and dementia rates climbing, a higher life expectancy may not be a total source of joy.

Medical standards will continue to improve, as they have over the last hundred years, not only in treatment or surgery, but in diagnosis. It is now possible to forecast the risk of future illnesses from your DNA, and you need only one drop of blood or a pinprick to diagnose many types of illness, cancer included. Whether all populations will get proper access to medical services is just as important as diagnosis and many societies will continue to fall short. To what extent medical pioneers will be able to create human tissue or try to clone human beings, as they cloned Dolly the sheep in 1996 and are now creating human-monkey embryos, will probably have to wait until the next time segment… Meanwhile, microbiologists will get a better understanding of the molecular mechanism underlying eukaryotic cellular processes and also the role and importance of bacteria. DNA sequencing will continue to advance although this does pose a risk, as it may lead to genomic intervention, which could be abused.

There will be continued development in computer technology, even picking up human brainwaves, whilst it is believed that artificial intelligence (AI) will match human intelligence within a hundred years. Also, AI will get better able to calculate, analyse, predict and discover. However, I believe the exponential increase in computer power, doubling every eighteen months, called Moore's law, will slow down. Industrial technology will continue to develop, driven by robotics, lasers and CD printing, miniaturising both plant and assembly tools down to a microscopic level, and speeding up production. In warehouses too, collaborative robots will change the face of distribution. Outside in the countryside, farming will become more mechanical, and hydroponic farming will increase, needing neither fields nor soil but using aqueous solutions. Less chemicals will be needed and some land will return to rewilding.

Together with the loss of clerical jobs, taken over by digital or quantum computers, this will lead to a rise in unemployment or a reduction in working hours or four-day working. However, not all employment will be affected as new businesses will take their place. For example, there will be an increase in IT, marketing, research, programming, risk analysis, medical services, personal care, travel, leisure pursuits, and all the arts, and there will be a decrease in the number of low skilled workers. Digital payments will become the norm and some societies will become cashless, possibly with their citizens receiving a Universal Basic Income.

Most personal habits in terms of socialising, sports, gardening, eating, cooking, watching television and drinking alcohol are likely to stay the same, but working from home and shopping online, spurred on by the recent pandemic, will assuredly increase. Food consumption will change, with some moving to a more vegetarian diet, and consuming less meat or switching to cultured meat. This means less cattle, which would be good for climate change. However, the increased use of computers, smart phones, apps, and social media, particularly by the young, is going to change personal behaviour. There is also the danger that a voluntary app or digital ID providing personal information could give government or other bodies control over the population. Crime and fraud will continue as it always has, and it is hard to see prison populations being significantly reduced, unless cannabis is legalised, as so much crime is based on drugs.

Personal transport will change as we phase out fossil fuels to avoid pollution. Cars will fly from rooftops and urban airports, pilotless planes will transform travel and more trains will be high speed. Planes will use different fuels, including hydrogen and batteries, to fly more economically or faster. Energy needed for transport, heating and industry will still need nuclear power, however unpopular, although the supply of uranium will run out in due course. It is obvious that far more renewables are needed if fossil fuels are phased out. The opportunity to expand production of solar power in Africa, the Middle East and all tropical regions stares us in the face, whilst ocean and river power, using tides or waves, will hopefully be realised, just as dams were developed in the past.

The risk of conflict will remain with us over the next hundred years, whether due to political or religious differences, international competition or thirst for power. Sadly, wars, revolutions and terrorism have always been with us and weapons have developed apace. Looking back to the First World War, we used Lee-Enfield rifles, whereas in the Second World War we used atomic bombs! So, armies will get smaller and more high-tech. Tanks will fade out and swarms of armed drones or pilotless planes will take their place. Aircraft will become supersonic. Apart from aircraft carriers, large naval vessels will give way to small unmanned vessels carrying ballistic or other weapons. Troops will be able to use air-jets to manoeuvre. Nations will concentrate more on defence rather than offence, as it could take only one nuclear war to wipe out the human race. However, some nations or groups will wage economic and political warfare using cyber operations to knock out their opponents' power grids and sophisticated software.

I expect there will be minor wars and skirmishes in the next hundred years, though I think we have sufficient awareness of the risks to avoid another world war in this period. However, I have no confidence that one can be avoided in the next thousand years.

Looking at other risk factors over the next hundred years, we will continue to have pandemics. At the time of writing, over three million reported global deaths from Covid 19, which could be two or three times higher, seems alarming. But we should put that into context with death rates in the past. One third of the European population died in the Black Death in 1347 and fifty million people died from Spanish flu in 1918 to 1920. It is also estimated that as many as 300 million people died from smallpox throughout the whole of the twentieth century. The current respiratory illness may well be curable or vaccinatable, but another pandemic will surely come along, hopefully not as severe as in the past.

Apart from pandemics, there are other risks of laboratory accidents, faulty manipulation of pathogens, contamination from earthly or spatial sources, or the spread of biological weapons, like Novichok, which is currently produced in Russia.

We now come to global warming with dire forecasts for rising sea levels, floods, forest fires, drought and famine which is likely to cause conflict over resources, water in particular, and may lead to displacement of people in some areas. Famine is always a risk, as China found out in Chairman Mao's 'Great Leap Forward.' But in future, it should only affect relatively small economies.

The emission of greenhouse gasses, principally carbon dioxide and the more damaging methane, is currently rising at the rate of one-fifth of one per cent per decade, something that is thought to return earth to the hothouse state that existed 45 million years ago. However, we should bear in mind that, in the Cambrian period, average temperatures were 50 °c to 60 °c, falling to 20 °c in the Jurassic period, with carbon dioxide levels over ten times higher than they are today. Yet evolution still carried on.

Nonetheless, serious efforts are now being made to reduce carbon emissions, supported now by almost all countries. With coal phased out, an increase in electric cars, hydrogen-powered planes, reduced pollution from industry, less deforestation, less cattle herds and more photosynthetic plants, global emissions can be curbed, if not eliminated. In particular, we can cut down on methane emissions, ten times more potent than carbon dioxide, by reducing leaks from coal mines, oil wells and gas plants. So, I do not believe emissions and pollution will get out of hand in this period, which some believe will happen by 2050. But it cannot be ruled out in the next period.

Perhaps the most fascinating development, space exploration, will occur in the next 100 years, which H G Wells would certainly have approved of. Commercial operators like Elon Musk and Jeff Bezos have now entered the field, alongside national programmes to set up stations on the moon, Mars, and other planets. The aim is firstly to see that it can be done, just like conquering Everest, next to find a new source of minerals and finally, to establish a base for humans, should earth become uninhabitable.

However, despite all the current enthusiasm for space adventure and international rivalry, it is going to be a vast endeavour. The cost may come down but it will still be very, very expensive, and risky too. The moon looks pretty barren with a day time temperature of 120 °c at its equator and a thin atmosphere. Venus has a temperature of 465 °c. Mars has an atmosphere of 95 per cent carbon dioxide, which would promote plant growth but would not be any good for humans. There is very low gravity on Mars as it does not have an iron core like earth, the temperature ranges from minus 153 °c at the poles to plus 70 °c in the summer, and it would take nine months with current propulsion systems to get there. The landscape is mountainous, the only water is ice and severe dust storms sweep the planet. It is true that microbial life may have existed there in the past, but there is no certainty that evolution could develop there as it did on earth and that took four billion years.

Despite the cost, the risks and the forbidding atmospheres described above, there is no doubt that some progress will be made towards interplanetary travel. Claims are currently being made that humans will be able to land on Mars and mine asteroids for their metals in this century, but I think this is going too far too quickly. During this time segment we should be able to build bigger space stations, introduce space tourism - for whatever reason - send robot probes to Mars, even establish a small robot settlement there, and establish a base camp on our own moon. But, to establish a base on another planet or another moon where water is available, oxygen can be made available, temperature can be controlled, radiation can be avoided, astronauts can walk around without spacesuits, and food can be produced on site, is going to have to wait until the next time segment.

Meanwhile, we must solve the problem of spacecraft propulsion. Current rocket fuels are inadequate for long-distance travel for humans to reach planets other than the moon. Whilst we can propel rockets at ten times the speed of sound, we need to reach one-tenth the speed of light to reach other planets inside or beyond the solar system. There are currently a number of propulsion systems being studied or tested that are said to produce sufficient acceleration in space, sustainable by astronauts, including sail-ships with enormous mesh sails energised by laser beams, ion engines and thrusters, nuclear fusion rockets and gamma ray photon fusion rockets. So, let's see first which one actually works!

I have commented in Chapter 2 about the likelihood of life on other planets, given that there are one trillion galaxies and two trillion, trillion stars, each with their own planets. But there is no chance of meeting any of them in this time segment - unless you believe in unidentified flying objects (UFOs) getting here first!

CHAPTER 7

THE NEXT THOUSAND YEARS

It is likely that the population will grow very gradually in the next thousand years, not fast enough to incur Malthus' theory of diminishing resources per head but, hopefully, matching a gradual increase in resources. If that happens, gross international product should increase in line and poverty will diminish, even if the disparity between rich and poor remains. As for democracy, it has already lasted over a thousand years despite wars, revolution, totalitarian leaders, terrorism and periodic restrictions of liberty. This sounds as though it could be a Goldilocks' environment, but I believe it will be interrupted by pandemics, fierce international competition, war, terrorism and accidents as yet unknown. The earth itself will continue, even if asteroids must be diverted, or giant eruptions occur, like Mount Toba 75,000 years ago which piled thirty feet of ash onto some areas of the planet.

It is hard to envisage how offensive and defensive weapons will develop beyond the first hundred years which were described in the previous chapter. In previous millennia, weapons developed slowly from bows to swords to chariots. Now that we have atomic bombs, nuclear submarines and ballistic weapons, there is not much more needed to kill off an enemy, so I believe much of weapon design will be on defence so that we are not obliterated by a rogue power. Nonetheless, the risk of world war cannot be ignored. Discontent and the need for change or reform can start from small beginnings and through either a political process or a revolution, it can lead to a dictatorial regime. If a major war does break out, wiping out a majority of the world's population, I believe the shock would be sufficient to lead the survivors to form a group like the League of Nations, working together to guarantee future peace.

Technology will continue to improve, both in manufacture and computing. Industry will continue to miniaturise, moving from microscopic to nanoscopic and molecular production. Robots will do much of the work and there is no limit to what they can achieve. As they get more sophisticated we may worry they will become more intelligent than us humans. But, as long as they are not self-aware and do not have life experience like us, there should be no danger. However, by the end of another thousand years, I believe that robots will be able to self-replicate under our control.

With a growing population, continuing industry and advanced transport, we will definitely need more energy, and we will still have to make use of nuclear power, until uranium runs out, together with solar power, wind power, hydrogen power and whatever fossil fuels are still available. We should also have developed nuclear fusion early in this time segment, fusing atoms of deuterium and tritium at over 100 million degrees Celsius to deliver ten times the energy put in. I would also be astonished if we do not make far more use of solar power, as sunlight delivers more energy to the earth in one hour than mankind currently uses in one year!

An enlarged population will still need food and this will put more pressure on agriculture, not only to increase supplies but to produce food more economically, using both current and hydroponic growing systems.

Individuals should need to work less, allowing more time for sport and leisure activities. As for our health, medical advances will increase exponentially. There will be experiments in creating human tissue, transplanting eukaryotic cell nuclei into host egg cells, and cloning of animals. I hope this does not include cloning humans, which is banned at present, but some pioneers are still likely to try it out. Obviously great strides are likely in the diagnostic capability of DNA and various new treatments that follow. But I am concerned about the possible creation and transfer of neurons into the brain, which could be abused. Whether this all keeps us alive longer has yet to be seen. Average age, not potential maximum age, could exceed 120, but I do not believe it will exceed 150 in this segment of time, even if resuscitation after death has been achieved or anti-ageing pills are successful. New epidemics will still occur, but it will kill off only a small percentage of the population each time.

Global warming will gradually continue and I do not believe it can be entirely contained, even if we become carbon neutral. However, I do not think this would be a sufficient catastrophe to wipe out the human race. As I commented in the last chapter, evolution continued with vastly higher levels of carbon dioxide in earlier paleontological periods, even if there was no additional pollution at that time.

Finally, we come to exploration. As long as mankind is imbued with a sense of wanderlust, we are not going to halt the search for extra-terrestrial life and the need for another location in space in case our own earth becomes uninhabitable. There are now hundreds of astronomers, scientists, engineers and physicists, as well as bodies like NASA, looking at ways to reach and inhabit another planet. The planets we have looked at so far seem to be uninhabitable and both the risks and the time taken to get there currently make it look too difficult.

But that is now. There is no scientific reason why robots cannot land on another planet, mine for supplies of materials and build structures for living. The only question is whether humans can live there, carry on breeding and enjoy the life style. If so, and as soon as we have solved the problem of accelerating propulsion, built suitable spacecraft, and worked out how to provide satisfactory living conditions on another planet, we can look farther than Mars to moons like Europa or Titan, or to other moons round Jupiter and Saturn. If successful, we could then look at planets outside the solar system, in particular, the triple star system named Alpha Centauri, the nearest star to the sun, where we are told conditions are more favourable than on our own planets.

In the meantime, let us hope that no-one has pressed the nuclear button.

CHAPTER 8

THE NEXT MILLION YEARS

One million years is just a speck in time in evolutionary terms. When we look back, we think in terms of paleontological periods with new species of animals emerging, periodic extinctions and changes in climate. It is over one billion years since the eukaryotic cell emerged, essential for life. So, I believe that if *homo sapiens* had not emerged, life would just carry on just as before. What *sapiens* has done, with all his new inventions, is to speed up the changes and alter the whole balance of risk. Indeed, one is fearful that some fatal incident could occur, not just in the next million, but even in the next thousand years.

Should an accident occur or world war breaks out, there is always the hope that civilisation could continue on another planet. Whilst I am not certain that we shall still be inhabiting earth in a million years, I am sure we will not be worrying about our longevity, the growth in global population, or health, wealth and happiness. As for space travel, mankind is certainly clever enough to find and settle on another planet, which we discussed in the previous chapter, possibly leapfrogging from one planet to another farther away, using lack of gravity to assist take-off.

As for future risks, these have to be split into catastrophic and existential. Every 100,000 years or so the sun moves further away from earth, which could lead to another ice age.

When we looked back at the evolution of animals we saw that over 99 per cent of animal species have become extinct at one time or another. So, who can say that our own species will not go the same way? Only *australopithecus africanus* is believed to have lasted longer than one million years.

In the meantime, there are some threats that we know about, as they have happened before. These include climate change, freezing or overheating, greenhouse gasses, severe volcanic eruptions or an asteroid hitting earth. Both the Arctic and Antarctic could disappear as we know them, or the world could get glacial, even if mankind found a way to keep going. Tectonic plates will continue moving, subverting continents, although that would not extinguish life. There is also bound to be one or more Carrington events with geomagnetic storms, throwing off billions of tons of charged particles, slamming into the earth's atmosphere and knocking out all electric grids, essential for living. In space there is also the threat that two super massive black holes which form the nucleus of galaxies could collide, causing, we are told, an explosion sufficient to wipe out a number of stars.

The biggest fear, I think, must be global warfare in which a rogue ruler, seeking domination, or trying to obtain scarce resources in order to survive, triggers a nuclear conflagration. In this event, only self-aware robots could continue.

CHAPTER 9

OVER ONE MILLION YEARS

Just as life would almost certainly continue for a million years without the advent of *homo sapiens*, it would probably continue for a hundred million years or longer. There would certainly be risks ahead, whether or not mankind was present, but you would need more than H G Wells' prophetic vision at this point in time to assess which incident was likely to arise, or what other changes could occur. In the end, only one thing is certain and that is the sun will eventually run out of fuel and the solar system will collapse.

I have set out below the principal risks or developments, not in any order, which I can foresee after one million years have passed, for you to consider. What I have not done is to assess the probability of any of these occurring. To find out more about the assessment of some of the risks, you ca n turn to the Future of Humanity Institute at Oxford University.

The Risks or Changes

1. Severe arctic freeze.

2. Large asteroid hitting earth.

3. Unknown virus pandemic.

4. Global warming, raised carbon dioxide and methane levels.

5. Super-volcanic eruption, magma extrusion and sulphur emissions.

6. Agriculture no longer viable.

7. Energy resources run out.

8. Social collapse.

9. Concentration of all populations into one world order.

10. Settlement or civilisation on another planet.

11. Radiation from collapsed supernova.

12. Catastrophic solar storm.

13. Contamination from outer space.

14. Final nuclear war.

15. Germ warfare or poisoning.

16. Extreme genetic mutation of humans.

17. Visit or attack from other planets.

18. Settlement on another planet.

19. Control by self-aware robots.

20. AI system takes control.

21. Evolution of new *homo species* (such as *floresiensis*).

22. Extinction of *homo sapiens*.

23. Collision of black holes.

24. So-called 'inflation' reverses.

25. New Big Bang.

I rest my case! It's now up to you to consider what comes next!

Printed in the United States
by Baker & Taylor Publisher Services